New Perspectives in H.

WHY HITLER?

Edited by

AMOS E. SIMPSON
University of Southwestern Louisiana

with the assistance of

SARAH CAIN NEITZEL
University of Southwestern Louisiana

Houghton Mifflin Company · **Boston**

New York · *Atlanta* · *Geneva, Illinois* · *Dallas* · *Palo Alto*

Printed in the U.S.A.

Library of Congress Catalog Card Number: 76-130656

ISBN: 0-395-11072-6

"In the course of the last 25 years, the soul of our people has been poisoned by jingoism to such an extent that our people would probably become cowards if deprived of such arrogant self-praise."

Chancellor Bethmann-Hollweg to Chief of the Imperial Civil Cabinet von Valentini, March, 1915, quoted in Erich Eyck, *A History of the Weimar Republic*, translated by Harlan P. Hanson and Robert G. L. Waite (Cambridge, Massachusetts: Harvard University Press, 1962), I, 1.

Contents

Introduction

U. S. Ambassador George C. McGhee recently said, "The time has come, I say, for the world to make up its mind about the Germans. I say this because there is evidence that many have not made up their minds. I say this because I believe that ample grounds for a decision exist."

The ambassador's points are well-taken. The Germans have worked hard for acceptance for the past twenty years, and in many respects the nation has achieved recognition as a partner in the Western Community of nations. Yet the student of German and world history must be aware that distrust of the Germans exists, and that "Time does not change the facts of the Nazi past, nor lighten its oppressive weight upon the history of humanity." Only when we can understand how and why Adolf Hitler and the Nazis came to authoritarian power, however, will we be able to follow the ambassador's suggestions.

Documentation abounds. Probably no other phenomenon in history is so fully documented for the general public as is the Nazi era in Germany. The victorious powers collected records for the trial of the German leaders as war criminals, and vast volumes have been published. Other and greater numbers of documents were boxed and stored for future reference. The number of memoirs and autobiographies is phenomenal. They began with the apologies of the Social Democrats immediately after 1933, and were sharply augmented after 1945 as those who were Nazis or Nazi supporters felt it necessary to justify their positions. Newspapers, journals, radio, propaganda techniques, all were available and useful in preserving the record.

The documentary record is not enough, however, to explain "Why Hitler?" Perhaps it would be enough if the record supported the Army-Big Business Conspiracy theory. But it won't. The German people established Hitler and the Nazis in power through conscious action and conscious inaction. Our problem then is to ascertain as accurately as possible, *why* this should be so.

Our failure to arrive at a decision does not stem from a dearth of effort. Historians, economists, journalists, constitutional lawyers, and psychiatrists have bent their efforts in this direction. But there is little agreement among them. Often the bitterness generated during the war years and the consciousness of the mass slaughter of 6,000,000 human beings without even the justification of war preclude an objective viewpoint. But even objective studies still must wrestle with the problem of how much weight to give to individual factors. Some argue that any nation, having experienced the losses attendant upon military defeat in World War I, having suffered the greatest inflation the world has known, having lifted itself through discipline into economic viability again only to face the unemployment crisis of the Great Depression, might well have responded in the same way. The opponents of this school point out that much of what happened to Germany was brought on by her own policies, policies peculiarly German.

Part of the confusion stems from the fact that the so-called revolution of 1918 was really no revolution at all. The real power in Germany prior to 1918 was vested in the army, the bureaucracy, the landlords, and the industrialists. The majority of the German people identified these groups with the nation.

Loss of the war discredited the leadership, and the old system should have been destroyed by the 1918 revolution. Such was not, in fact, the case. The Emperor and the monarchy were blamed for causing and losing the war, and monarchy was legally abolished. But the power factors were not destroyed because of fear of invasion, fear of Bolshevism, fear of, in fact, social revolution. Most Germans were too eager for place, prestige, order, and security to support social revolution.

The Social Democratic Party split over this matter, with the extreme left wing, under the leadership of Karl Liebknecht and Rosa Luxembourg, refusing to vote for credits to finance the war as early as 1914. This group came to be known as the Spartacist Union, and after 1919 Communists. A bit more moderate in their aims were the Independent Socialists who split off from the main party in 1917 over the war aims. The majority of the Social Democrats, however, refused to support destruction of the power of the army, the bureaucracy, the landlords, or the industrialists when the revolution came in 1918.

The other party not formally committed to the preservation of the establishment was the Catholic Center. Because it included so many social and economic levels, its ideological values were diverse. Yet the Center, too, was unwilling to participate in the disruption of the power factors. Many of its leaders were industrialists, and too many others were members for religious rather than social, political or economic reasons.

The Democratic Party came into existence only with the revolution. It was the only party committed to the democratization of Germany under a republican form of government. But its support declined in every election from 1919 through 1932, and it managed to elect only two members to the Reichstag in the latter years. The other parties, both right and left, either actively opposed a democratic republic or remained non-committed.

In the eight elections held during the fourteen years of the Weimar Republic's life, no party ever received a clear majority. The numerous governments which held office during the period were, therefore, all coalition governments. There was a consistent movement from left to right as cabinet changes took place. From the moment of the proclamation of the Republic its leaders engaged in collusion with the right-wing elements to prevent any real revolution of the Left. Friedrich Ebert made a deal on November 10, 1918, with the Officers' Corps. The new government would leave the army alone if the army would help it destroy the Independent Socialists and the Spartacists, and their followers among the radical workers. In 1918 and 1919 the army thus killed several thousand workers who were too radical to please the Social Democratic leadership.

At the same time the army refused to protect the established government against right-wing attacks. Early in 1920 the government was forced out of Berlin by Free Corps elements with the active support of the local army commander, and the tacit support of the chief of staff.Only a general strike saved the government at that time.

Adolf Hitler and his followers attempted their Beer-Hall Putsch on November 8, 1923. The major leaders were never punished at all for this violent attempt to overthrow the government. True, Hitler was given the best living quarters he had ever known for a few months, and with the secretarial help of Rudolf Hess, wrote *Mein Kampf.* On an earlier occasion (in 1919) a left-wing attempt to overthrow the government had resulted in the ruthless liquidation of all concerned, along with many innocent people. From the inception of the Weimar Republic, then, those who were supposed to be its strongest supporters, those who had the responsibility of protecting it, aligned themselves with the forces determined to overthrow the new government.

Especially significant among the forces which signally failed the Weimar Republic was the judiciary. During the crucial years numerous, and now almost forgotten, small right-wing groups formed specifically for purposes of lawlessness and violence against the Republic and its leaders. But even-handed justice simply did not exist. The members of the judiciary and magistracy were holdovers from the imperial regime. They held an active bias against any person or organization which was left of center, and an equally active bias for right-wing violators of law and constitution. This obvious double standard encouraged lawlessness from both sides. The right-wing elements needed not fear punishment; the left-wing protagonists had no recourse except violence.

The state of Bavaria was among the worst examples of right-wing determination to overthrow the young government. It was to the capital city of Munich that Adolf Hitler returned after the war, and was employed by the Reichswehr as an "education officer." Here, too, were Ludendorff, Gottfried Feder, Dietrich Eckart, and Anton Drexler, among large numbers of secret organizations, Free Corps men, anti-republican publications, and right-wing judges.

As part of his work for the Reichswehr, Hitler joined the German Workers' Party, headed by Anton Drexler, in July 1919. At that time the party was well-nigh indistinguishable from a dozen others. Some forty members met to agree that the war was not over, that the lower classes were mistreated, and that all Germans should be part of Germany. Under Drexler's leadership that is all it could ever have been. He believed he was right, and that therefore his ideas would spread without effort. Hitler, on the other hand, added the will to power, and the techniques of virulent propaganda.

In 1920 a committee composed of Hitler, Feder, Eckart, and Drexler wrote a party platform which was designed to have a broad appeal. Its purpose was to catch all who were opposed to the Republic. Shortly thereafter the party name was changed to broaden the base. It became the National Socialist German Workers' Party. Then in 1921 Hitler managed to get the leadership principle established with himself as absolute leader. The militant arm was provided by the Storm Troops. Money to support them and the party often came through Hitler's violation of the "unalterable" twenty-five point program. To industrialists and landowners Hitler explained that the expropriation proposals against them in the program referred only to Jewish property and capital.

But we must remember that in the early years growth of the party was slow. There were probably fewer than 15,000 members when the Putsch was attempted in 1923, and in 1928 the Nazis elected only twelve members to the Reichstag. Some other factor must help explain the rise to power. That additional factor is the world depression following 1929. Following hard on the Wall Street crash in October 1929, Germany's sources of credit dried up. Much of her apparent economic success after the inflation of 1923 had rested on foreign credits. Rationalization of her industry had already reduced purchasing power at home. The depression and increasing tariffs reduced foreign markets. Unemployment increased sharply, and among the hardest hit were the lower middle class, fixed-income people.

Here class pride enters the picture. In Germany poverty to the middle class is much more than merely going hungry. The stigma attached to loss of place is perhaps more damaging. German voters reacted by a polarization to the two extremes of politics—the Nazis on the right, the Communists on the left. In the July 1930 elections the Nazis increased their Reichstag seats from twelve to 107. The Communists gained from fifty-four to seventy-seven.

The Brüning cabinet could not attain a working coalition which would produce a majority, but remained in power because the Social Democrats refused to join a vote of no-confidence. Government, then, was by presidential decree, and President Hindenburg with his coterie of followers was not inclined to rule in the interests of preserving the Republic. Indeed the old man (eighty-three years old) was senile to an advanced degree, and was easily controlled by his son Colonel Oskar, Colonel von Papen, Dr. Otto Meissner, General Kurt von Schleicher, and his neighbor Elard von Oldenburg-Januschau. These men represented the army, the landlords, and industry as well as themselves.

Von Papen convinced Hindenburg that by cutting off financial support to the Nazis, Hitler could be brought into line in a coalition government. The November election in 1932 proved part of his contention. The absence of financial support from industrial circles reduced the Nazis from 230 Reichstag seats to 196. Hitler agreed to accept the Chancellorship with only two other Nazis in a cabinet of eleven members. The rest of the contention, bringing Hitler into line, was a miserable failure. Within eighteen months, Hitler was Germany's master.

No time was wasted. Hitler was Chancellor. Wilhelm Frick, as Minister of the Interior, controlled the Federal police power. Frick was a Nazi. Hitler got Hindenburg to sign a decree removing Prussian ministers from office, and appointed his own men. Hermann Göring was given control of the Prussian police. While Hitler, Frick, and Göring attacked under the guise of legality from above, the Storm Troops under Röhm attacked with sheer force from below. Pitched battles developed as Röhm undertook to prevent any meeting of any party except the Nazi. He and his men were protected by the removal of any officials who opposed them.

Even so, Hitler feared he would show too little strength in the elections he had called for March 5, 1933. The Reichstag was burned, and the Communists were blamed in order to play on the fears of the masses, and in order to weaken the entire left of German politics. Immediately a decree suspended all civil liberties, and all Communist Reichstag members, with thousands of other Communists, were arrested. All Communist and Social Democratic newspapers were banned until after the election. Even so, the Nazis garnered only 43.9% of the total vote, but Hitler drove ahead with his "coordination" policy. The Storm Troops went on a protected rampage, destroying the offices and headquarters and plants of opposition parties, trade unions, publishers, even municipal governments. Their protection came from the appointment of Nazis to over-riding positions of power throughout Germany.

The disappointing election returns did not actually prevent the Nazis from majority control when the Reichstag met. All eighty-one Communist members were excluded, along with some thirty members of the Social Democrats. But to pass the Enabling Act which Hitler demanded required a two-thirds majority. Had the Center Party joined the Social Democrats, the Enabling Act would have failed. No doubt Hitler would have attempted something else, but opposition at that time would have stood much greater chance of success than later. Even President Hindenburg might have opposed blatant violence against constitutional procedures, and the army was not yet under Hitler's control as it was the following year.

The Enabling Act gave Hitler the power to destroy political parties, and in less than four months all except the Nazi Party had disappeared. Labor organizations, agricultural associations, religious bodies, all came under the coordination policies, and by 1934 were controlled.

The final step came with Hitler's destruction of the Storm Troops and the entire left wing of the Nazi Party on June 30, 1934. The authoritarian regime was established.

This regime holds the primary responsibility for World War II. It was guilty of deliberate mass murder of some 6,000,000 human beings, the routine practice of slave labor, and other horrors in such numbers that their mere cataloging weakens the force of the documentation. The primary purpose of this book is to present the reader with a collection of data, with contemporary evaluations, with various historical judgements, and with suggested reading lists, to enable him better to decide for himself how this twentieth century phenomenon came to be.

I German National Character

Germany entered on her experiment in democracy after World War I with almost no previous experience in the democratic process, and perhaps more importantly, little concept of the meaning of that process as Americans and Englishmen understand the term. Historians have reached little agreement concerning the reasons for the failure of the democratic experiment. The various explanations range from assertions that the Nazi era was the inevitable and ultimate expression of an inherent viciousness in the German character to statements that the whole episode was nothing more than an historical accident.

The selections we have chosen reflect an attempt to depict some of the more moderate interpretations while retaining the divergent points of view concerning the German mentality. Some delve deep into the German past to find basic attitudes which explain the need for a strong Leader. Others find causation in more recent events. Some place responsibility directly on the German people as a whole, others blame that amorphous entity "The West," while still others have attempted to select some segment of society, or some aspect of *Deutschtum* to bear the onus of guilt.

The governmental system which preceded the Weimar Republic was established by Prince Otto von Bismarck. It came to be accepted by every important element of German society. Bismarck's ideas, then, may be taken as reflective of the collective Will of the German people after 1871. The other selections are chosen to exemplify more recent German and Western scholarship.

OTTO VON BISMARCK

Memoirs

Imperial Germany, it is true, had a constitution with some democratic elements. But the absence of the spirit of true parliamentary government may be read in the words of the creator of the Empire and its constitution. Prince Otto von Bismarck in his *Memoirs* wrote specifically on this subject. The Constitution as it was given to Germany by Bismarck reflected his statement that he preferred a dictatorship to a parliamentary government. He prevented the establishment of a representative government and thus prevented the German people from gaining any experience in government.

THE IDEA of the King's abdication was fresh to me when I was received at Babelsberg on September 22, [1862] and the situation only became clear to me when his Majesty defined it in some such words as these: "I will not reign if I cannot do it in such a fashion as I can be answerable for to God, my conscience, and my subjects. But I cannot do that if I am to rule according to the will of the present majority in parliament, and I can no longer find any ministers prepared to conduct my government without subjecting themselves and me to the parliamentary majority. I have therefore resolved to lay down my crown, and have already sketched out the proclamation of my abdication, based on the motives to which I have referred." The King showed me the document in his own handwriting lying on the table, whether already signed or not I do not know. His Majesty concluded by repeating that he could not govern without suitable ministers.

I replied that his Majesty had been acquainted ever since May with my readiness to enter the ministry; I was certain that Roon would remain with me on his side, and I did not doubt that we should succeed in completing the cabinet, supposing other members should feel themselves compelled to resign on account of my admission. After a good deal of consideration and discussion, the King asked me whether I was prepared as minister to advocate the reorganization of the army, and when I assented he asked me further whether I would do so in opposition to the majority in parliament and its resolutions. When I asserted my willingness, he finally

From Otto von Bismarck, *The Memoirs* (New York: 1899; Howard Fertig, Inc.: 1966).

declared, "Then it is my duty, with your help, to attempt to continue the battle, and I shall not abdicate." I do not know whether he destroyed the document which was lying on the table, or whether he preserved it *in rei memoriam.*

The King invited me to accompany him into the park. During the walk he gave me a programme to read, which filled eight pages of his close writing, embraced all eventualities of the politics of the time, and went into such details as the reform of the district sub-Diets. I cannot say whether this elaboration had already served as the basis of discussion with my predecessors, or whether it was to serve as a security against a policy of conservative thoroughness such as I was credited with. . . .

I succeeded in convincing him that, so far as he was concerned, it was not a question of Liberal or Conservative of this or that shade, but rather of monarchical rule or parliamentary government, and that the latter must be avoided at all costs, if even by a period of dictatorship. I said: "In this situation I shall, even if your Majesty command me to do things which I do not consider right, tell you my opinion quite openly; but if you finally persist in yours, I will rather perish with the King than forsake your Majesty in the contest with parliamentary government." This view was at that time strong and absolute in me, because I regarded the negations and phrases of the Opposition of that day as politically disastrous in face of the national task of Prussia, and because I cherished such strong feelings of devotion and affection for William I, that the thought of perishing with him appeared to me, under the circumstances, a natural and congenial conclusion to my life.

The King tore the programme to pieces, and was about to throw them down from the bridge into the dry ditch in the park, when I reminded him that these papers in his well-known writing might fall into very wrong hands. He saw that I was right, put the pieces in his pocket to commit them to the flames, and on the same day ratified my appointment as minister and interim chairman of the ministry, which was made public on the 23rd. The King kept my nomination as President in reserve, until he had completed the correspondence on the subject with Prince von Hohenzollern, who still occupied this post constitutionally.

CARROLL QUIGLEY
Tragedy and Hope

Support for the Bismarckian system was readily found among the German people. The following selection from Carroll Quigley's *Tragedy and Hope* develops his argument that from the time of the disintegration of the German tribal system in the early Middle Ages the German people have longed for the single allegiance, coziness, and security that a totalitarian state provides. The West, however, developed a pluralistic system in which the individual ranks above society. But the Germans hated such a system in which man is driven to making decisions, which requires self-reliance and rationalism.

THE FATE of Germany is one of the most tragic in all human history, for seldom has a people of such talent and accomplishment brought such disasters on themselves and on others. The explanation of how Germany came to such straits cannot be found by examining the history of the twentieth century alone. Germany came to the disaster of 1945 by a path whose beginnings lie in the distant past, in the whole pattern of German history from the days of the Germanic tribes to the present. That Germany had a tribal and not a civilized origin and was outside the boundaries of the Roman Empire and of the Latin language were two of the factors which led Germany ultimately to 1945. The Germanic tribe gave security and meaning to each individual's life to a degree where it almost absorbed the individual in the group, as tribes usually do. It gave security because it protected the individual in a social status of *known* and relatively stable social relationships with his fellows; it gave meaning because it was all-absorbing—totalitarian, if you will, in that it satisfied almost all an individual's needs in a single system.

The shattering of the Germanic tribe in the period of the migrations, fifteen hundred years ago, and the exposure of its members to a higher, but equally total and equally satisfying, social structure—the Roman imperial system; and the subsequent, almost immediately subsequent, shattering of that Roman system caused a double trauma from which the Germans have not recovered even today. The shattering of the tribe left the individual German, as a similar experience today has left many Africans, in a chaos of unfamiliar experiences in which there was neither security nor meaning. When all other relationships had been destroyed, the German was left with only one human relationship on which he turned all his energy—loyalty to his immediate companions. But this could not carry all his life's energy or satisfy all of life's needs—no single human relationship ever can—and the effort to make it do so can only turn it into a monstrosity. But the German tribesman of the sixth century, when all else was shattered, made such an effort and tried to build all security and all meaning on personal loyalty. Any violence, any criminal act, any bestiality was justified for the sake of the allegiance of personal loyalty. The result is to be seen in the earliest work of Germanic literature—the *Niebelungenlied,* a madhouse dominated by this one mood, in a situation not totally unlike the Germany of 1945.

Into the insanity of monomania created by the shattering of the Germanic tribes came the sudden recognition of a better system, which could be, they thought, equally secure, equally meaningful, because equally total. This was symbolized by the word *Rome.* It is almost impossible for us, of the West and of today, imbued as we are with historical perspective and individualism, to see what Classical culture was like, and why it appealed to the Germans. Both may be summed up in the word "total." The Greek *polis,* like the Roman *imperium,* was total. We in the West have escaped the fascination of totalitarianism because we have in our tradition other elements—the refusal of the Hebrews to confuse God with the world, or religion with the state, and the realization that God is transcendental, and, accordingly, all other things must be, in some degree, incomplete and thus imperfect. We also have, in our tradition, Christ, who stood apart from the state and told his followers to "Render to Caesar the things which are Caesar's." And we have in our tradition the church of the catacombs, where clearly human values were neither united nor total, and were opposed to the state. The Germans, as later the Russians, escaped the full influence of these elements in the tradition of the West. The Germans and the Russians knew Rome only in its post-Constantine phase when the Christian emperors were seeking to preserve the totalitarian system of Dioclesian, but in a Christian rather than a pagan totalitarianism. This was the system the detribalized Germans glimpsed just before it also was shattered. They saw it as a greater, larger, more powerful entity than the tribe but with the same elements which they wanted to preserve from their tribal past. They yearned to become part of that imperial totalitarianism. They still yearn for it. Theodoric, the Ostrogoth (Roman Emperor, 489-526), saw himself as a Germanic Constantine. The Germans continued their refusal to accept this second loss, as the Latins and the Celts were prepared to do, and for the next thousand years the Germans made every effort to reconstruct the Christian *imperium,* under Charles V (Holy Roman Emperor, 1519-1555) as under Theodoric. The German continued to dream of that glimpse he had had of the imperial system before it sank—one, universal, total, holy, eternal, imperial, Roman. He refused to accept that it was gone, hating the small group who opposed its revival and despising the great mass who did not care, while regarding himself as the sole defender of values and righteousness who was prepared to sacrifice anything to restore that dream on earth. . . .

During that thousand years, the West developed a pluralistic system in which the individual was the ultimate good (and the ultimate philosophic reality), faced with the need to choose among many conflicting allegiances. Germany was dragged along in the same process, but unwillingly, and continued to yearn for a single allegiance which would be totally absorbing. This desire appeared in many Germanic traits, of which one was a continued love affair with Greece and Rome. Even today a Classical scholar does more of his reading in German than in any other language, although he rarely recognizes that he does so because the appeal of Classical culture to the Germans rested on its totalitarian nature, recognized by Germans but generally ignored by Westerners.

All the subsequent experiences of the German people, from the failure of Otto the Great in the tenth century to the failure of Hitler in the twentieth century, have served to perpetuate and perhaps to intensify the German thirst for the coziness of the totalitarian way of life. This is the key to German national character: in spite of all their talk of heroic behavior, what they really wanted has been coziness, freedom from the need to make decisions which require an independent, self-reliant individual constantly exposed to the chilling breeze of numerous alternatives. . . . Decision, which requires the evaluation of alternatives, drives man to individualism, self-reliance, and rationalism, all hateful qualities to Germanism. . . .

In an exposed position in central Europe, Germany found herself trapped between France, Russia, and the Hapsburg dominions and was unable to deal with her basic problems in her own fashion and on their merits. Accordingly, Germany obtained national unity only late and "by blood and iron," and never obtained democracy at all. It might be added that she also failed to achieve laissez faire or liberalism for the same reasons. In most countries democracy was achieved by the middle classes, supported by peasants and workers, in an attack on the monarchy supported by the bureaucracy and landed aristocracy. In Germany this combination never quite came off, because these various groups were reluctant to clash with one another in the face of their threatening neighbors. Instead, Germany's exposed frontiers made it necessary for the various groups to subordinate their mutual antagonisms and obtain unification at the price of a sacrifice of democracy, laissez faire, liberalism, and nonmaterial values. Unification for Germany was achieved in the nineteenth century, not by embracing but by repudiating the typical nineteenth-century values. Starting as a reaction against the assault of Napoleon in 1806, and repudiating the rationalism, cosmopolitanism, and humanitarianism of the Enlightenment, Germany achieved unity only by the following processes:

1. by strengthening the monarchy and its bureaucracy;
2. by strengthening the permanent, professional army;
3. by preserving the landlord class (the Junkers) as a source of personnel for both bureaucracy and army;
4. by strengthening the industrial class through direct and indirect state subsidy, but never giving it a vital voice in state policy;
5. by appeasing the peasants and workers through paternalistic economic and social grants rather than by the extension of political rights which would allow these groups to assist themselves.

The long series of failures by the Germans to obtain the society they wanted served only to intensify their desire for it. They wanted a cozy society with both security and meaning, a totalitarian structure which would be at the same time universal and ultimate, and which would so absorb the individual in its structure that he would never need to make significant decisions for himself. Held in a framework of known, satisfying, personal relationships, such an individual would be safe because he would be surrounded by fellows equally satisfied with their own positions, each feeling important from his membership in the greater whole.

Although this social structure was never achieved in Germany, and never could be achieved, in view of the dynamic nature of Western Civilization in which the Germans were a part, each German over the centuries has tried to create such a situation for himself in his immediate environment (at the minimum in his family or beer garden) or, failing that, has created German literature, music, drama, and art as vehicles of his protests at this lack. This desire has been evident in the German's thirst for status (which establishes his relationship with the whole) and for the absolute (which gives *unchanging* meaning to the whole).

The German thirst for status is entirely different from the American desire for status. The American is driven by the desire to get ahead, that is, to change his status; he wants status and status symbols to exist as clear evidence or even measures of the speed with which he is changing his status. The German wants status as a nexus of obvious relationships around himself so there will never be doubt in anyone's mind where he stands, stationary, in the system. He wants status because he dislikes changes, because he abhors the need to make decisions. The American thrives on change, novelty, and decisions. Strangely enough, both react in this opposite fashion for somewhat similar reasons based on the inadequate maturation and integration of the individual's personality. The American seeks change, as the German seeks *external* fixed relationships, as a distraction from the lack of integration, self-sufficiency, and internal resources of the individual himself.

The German wants status reflected in obvious external symbols so that his nexus of personal relationships will be clear to everyone he meets and so that he will be treated accordingly, and almost automatically (without need for painful decisions). He wants titles, uniforms, nameplates, flags, buttons, anything which will make his position clear to all. In every German organization, be it business, school, army, church, social club, or family, there are ranks, gradations, and titles. No German could be satisfied with just his name on a calling card or on the nameplate of his doorway. His calling card must also have his address, his titles, and his educational achievements. . . .

Such emphasis on position, precedence, titles, gradations, and fixed relationships, especially up and down, are so typically German that the German is most at home in hierarchical situations such as a military, ecclesiastical, or educational organization, and is often ill at ease in business or politics where status is less easy to establish and make obvious.

With this kind of nature and such neurological systems, Germans are ill at ease with equality, democracy, individualism, freedom and other features of modern life. Their neurological systems were a consequence of the coziness of German childhood, which, contrary to popular impression, was not a condition of misery and personal cruelty (as it often is in England), but a warm, affectionate, and externally disciplined situation of secure relationships. After all, Santa Claus and the child-centered Christmas is Germanic. This is the situation the adult German, face to face with what seems an alien world, is constantly seeking to recapture. To the German it is *Gemütlichkeit;* but to outsiders it may be suffocating. In any case it gives rise among adult Germans to two additional traits of German character: the need for external discipline and the equality of egocentricity.

The Englishman is disciplined from within so that he takes his self-discipline, embedded in his neurological system, with him wherever he goes, even to situations where all the external forms of discipline are lacking. As a consequence the Englishman is the most completely socialized of Europeans, as the Frenchman is the most completely civilized, the Italian most completely gregarious, or the Spaniard most completely individualistic. But the German by seeking external discipline shows his unconscious desire to recapture the externally disciplined world of his childhood. With such discipline he may be the best behaved of citizens, but without it he may be a beast.

A second notable carryover from childhood to adult German life was egocentricity. The whole world seems to any child to revolve around it, and most societies have provided ways in which the adolescent is disabused of this error. The German leaves childhood so abruptly that he rarely learns this fact of the universe, and spends the rest of his life creating a network of established relationships centering on himself. Since this is his aim in life, he sees no need to make any effort to see anything from any point of view other than his own. The consequence is a most damaging inability to do this. Each class or group is totally unsympathetic to any point of view except the egocentric one of the viewer himself. His union, his company, his composer, his poet, his party, his neighborhood are the best, almost the only acceptable, examples of the class, and all others must be denigrated. As part of this process a German usually chooses for himself his favorite flower, musical composition, beer, club, painting, or opera, and sees little value or merit in any other. Yet at the same time he insists that his myopic or narrow-angled vision of the universe must be universalized, because no people are more insistent on the role of the absolute or the universal as the framework of their own egocentricity. One deplorable consequence of this has been the social animosities rampant in a Germany which has loudly proclaimed its rigid solidarity.

With an individual personality structure such as this, the German was painfully uncomfortable in the totally different, and to him totally unfriendly, world of nineteenth-century individualism, liberalism, competitive atomism, democratic equality, and self-reliant dynamicism. And the German was doubly uncomfortable and embittered by 1860 to see the power, wealth, and national unity which these nineteenth-century traits had brought to Britain and France. The late arrival of these achievements, especially national unity and industrialism, in Germany left the average German with a feeling of inferiority in respect to England. Few Germans were willing to compete as individuals with British businessmen. Accordingly, the newly unified German government was expected to help German industrialists with tariffs, credit, price and production controls, cheaper labor costs, and such. As a consequence Germany never had a clearly competitive, liberal economy like the Western Powers. . . .

The dichotomy in Germany between appearance and reality, between propaganda and structure, between economic prosperity and political and social weakness was put to the test in World War I, and failed completely. The events of 1914-1919 revealed that Germany was not a democracy in which all men were legally equal. Instead, the ruling groups formed some strange animal lording it over a host of lesser animals. In this strange creature the monarchy represented the body, which was supported by four legs: the army, the landlords, the bureaucracy, and the industrialists.

This glimpse of reality was not welcome to any important group in Germany,with the result that it was covered over, almost at once, by another misleading facade: the "revolution" of 1918 was not really a revolution at all, because it did not radically change this situation; it removed the monarchy, but it left the quartet of legs. . . .

FRIEDRICH MEINECKE

The German Catastrophe

The German historian, Friedrich Meinecke, in contrast to Quigley, places more blame on the Western situation for the advent of Hitler. Nazi support came mainly from the bourgeoisie, according to Meinecke, but the bourgeoisie were a result of Western society and were not characteristic of German society. The bourgeois desire for profits, power, and comfortable living was an outgrowth of the Enlightenment and the French Revolution. When the Weimar Republic failed to fulfill that desire, the bourgeoisie, in a non-German fashion, accepted Hitler's promises to restore them to their Bismarckian role. The reader may note, however, in the following selection, that even while Meinecke is placing responsibility for the rise of the Nazis on non-German aspects of Western Civilization, he is himself guilty of a clear expression of that same anti-semitism which contributed so strongly to Hitler's rise.

THE QUESTION of the deeper causes of the frightful catastrophe which burst upon Germany will still occupy the coming centuries—provided these centuries are indeed still able and inclined to ponder problems of this kind. But then the question of the German catastrophe broadens at the same time to a question which extends beyond Germany to the destiny of the West in general. Hitler's National Socialism, which brought us directly to this abyss, is not a phenomenon deriving from merely German evolutionary Forces, but has also certain analogies and precedents in the authoritarian systems of neighboring countries, however horribly peculiar Nazism presents itself as an example of degeneration in the German character. But one asks further, how could this take place—this astonishing deviation from the main lines of a European development which was apparently moving toward some kind of free-individualistic and binding-collectivist elements making toward the preservation of the liberal gains of the nineteenth century? Instead of a liberal tendency there came the precipitate shift to despotism, the rise of the *terribles simplificateurs* whom Jakob Burckhardt more than half a century ago saw coming. Burckhardt, more clearsighted than any other thinker of his time, also gives the first answers to our problem, which he understood at its first appearance. In the optimistic illusions of the Age of Enlightenment and the French Revolution he already perceived the germ of the great disease—the mistaken striving after the unattainable happiness of the masses of mankind, which then shifted into a desire for profits, power, and a general striving for living well. So there came about, Burckhardt further observes, the loosening of old social ties and ultimately the creation of new but very powerful ties by those men of violence, those *terribles simplificateurs,* who, supported by military organizations, forced the masses back again into discipline and obedience and a renunciation of all their former longings for freedom. In the misery of their daily existence they could then be called to position every morning by the beat of the drum and in the evening be led home again by the beat of the drum.

It was thus as a Western, and not merely as a German problem— as the historical problem of a declining culture in general—that Burckhardt saw these things taking place. . . .

The degeneration of the German people is what we are here trying, by groping and probing, to understand merely in its rough outlines. How difficult it is, however, to sketch a picture of the spiritual and cultural condition of Germany in the first decades after the founding of the Empire in 1871, of the good as well as the bad germs in it. The judgment commonly expressed today, often merely parroting Nietzsche, that liberalism had become flat and shallow, settles nothing. The silver age of classical liberalism, of which we spoke, still persisted and still produced in art and science much that was brilliant, while the average level and everyday taste remained decidedly low. But no one then would have thought possible the emergence in educated Germany of a phenomenon like National Socialism—only the uneducated, proletarian Germany of Social Democracy was feared as a serious menace to our culture in the future. We, especially we younger Germans, felt exceedingly safe, entirely too safe, in the possession of a high national and cultural heritage. Here and there, however, clouds began to appear in this bright sky.

The anti-Semitic movement at the beginning of the eighties brought the first flash of lightning. The Jews, who were inclined to enjoy indiscreetly the favorable economic situation now smiling upon them, had since their full emancipation aroused resentment of various sorts. They contributed much to that gradual depreciation and discrediting of the liberal world of ideas that set in after the end of the nineteenth century. The fact that besides their negative and disintegrating influence they also achieved a great deal that was positive in the cultural and economic life of Germany was forgotten by the mass of those who now attacked the damage done by the Jewish character. Out of the anti-Semitic feeling it was possible for an anti-liberal and anti-humanitarian feeling to develop easily—the first steps toward National Socialism. In the popularity which the anti-Semitic rector Ahlwardt, a man of the crudest half-education, enjoyed in the early eighties, one can see the soft prelude to Hitler's later success. But people would have laughed if any one at that time had predicted to us such a success. We Germans felt all too secure in our firmly established state based on the reign of law, in our comfortable civil order, in our liberal ideals—still ever shining in spite of their paling—of freedom, self-determination, and human dignity.

The whole bourgeois world . . . was still borne along on one of the two waves which swept through the nineteenth century—the wave of the national movement. But this was crisscrossed . . . by the second great wave—the socialist movement which arose from the masses of the industrial proletariat. We shall limit ourselves here to the attempt to explain what this second movement, by its inherent tendencies as well as by its reaction upon the bourgeois world, may have meant for the rise of National Socialism.

The socialist state that was the goal of the future could be realized only as a state which was to a high degree authoritarian and which organized daily life thoroughly. It remained at first a dream of the future and the thinking of the masses was certainly more concerned with the needs, cares, and desires of daily life than with it. One may suspect, however, that it helped materially to collectivize the masses and to modify deeply their feeling about legal rights; that is, the rights of the individual grew dimmer and the rights of the total state over the individual were allowed to become continually stronger. The phrase "prison state" was flung in reproach at the socialists because that described, so it was said, what they were trying to set up. On the one hand, the anger and hate of those who felt exploited toward the other traditional social groups, who were regarded as reactionary, directly undermined the feeling for traditional historical authority in general. Hatred inflamed the revolutionary recklessness with which people trampled upon the rights and property of their opponents. So there developed a revolutionary spirit in general, to which National Socialism could later fall heir. The thing that was astonishing and characteristic of German development was the fact that this revolutionary spirit could change its bearers and could somehow leap from the class of the industrial proletariat, which had carried it hitherto, to other social classes now arising, some for the first time. . . .

There existed at the turn of the century a great deal of good old bourgeois culture which as a matter of course, in spite of the increasing superficiality of life, put certain moral restraints on political ambitions. . . . The two streams in the bourgeois camp met most closely in the field of world politics, in the demand for armed participation in the struggles for the partition of the world and for securing Germany's living space in the future. All the bourgeois elements merged together in the movement for building the navy, as to whose size, to be sure, people had no clear conception. In case of serious danger this merger of interests would have held together just as little as it held together during the First World War. Fundamentally the bad and the good mentors of the German bourgeoisie at this time were completely divorced.

Germany was not the only country into which the evil penetrated. One must say today that the whole imperialist movement of the Western nations was responsible for creating the conditions for the impending political as well as cultural disaster of the west, even though one may also recognize the inevitability of imperialism and its solicitude for the future of one's own people. Every requirement of this kind, however, bears within itself new germs of evil, and the extent of the evil depends essentially upon the measure of insight and caution in the intellectual and moral make-up of the leading circles among the people. No people had more reason to exercise caution and moderation than the Germans in their shut-in and endangered position and with their tendency to exaggerate ideas which they have once seized upon. We may quote here the words of a noble philosopher, Friedrich Paulsen, in 1902, also from the *Preussische Jahrbucher* (volume 110, page 173); they express the growing alarm of humaneminded patriots:

> A supersensitive nationalism has become a very serious danger for all the people of Europe; because of it, they are in danger of losing the feeling for human values. Nationalism, pushed to an extreme, just like sectarianism, destroys moral and even logical consciousness. Just and

unjust, good and bad, true and false, lose their meaning; what men condemn as disgraceful and inhuman when done by others, they recommend in the same breath to their own people as something to be done to a foreign country.

There you have the ethics of Hitler's National Socialism.

We have reached here only the first stages of the process of degeneration in the German bourgeoisie. The two decades prior to the outbreak of the First World War were an era of the strongest counterforces vying with one another and an era of uncertain possibilities for the future. . . . And however unconditionally the drive for wealth and power seemed to proceed in the managerial circles of this bourgeoisie, these two decades before the First World War were nevertheless filled at the same time with a new idealistic striving, with a renewing of ties with the Goethe golden age, ties which were by no means merely imitative but were also creative. A quite special, modern spirit arose, particularly in art and poetry. Truth, sincerity, and inwardness can be seen as the guiding stars of these new tendencies, often combined with a radical determination to break down on the way all restraint imposed by the previously existing world. At the same time, to be sure, there were the fatal threads of connection with the rising amoral nationalism with which we have become acquainted as the immediate prelude to Hitlerism. In Nietzsche's realm of ideas, which now began to exert a powerful influence over all yearning and restless spirits, there were gathered together almost all the noble and ignoble desires and self-longings which filled this period—a demonic phenomenon in the disruptiveness of its character and influence. It was predominantly harmful. Nietzsche's superman, destroying the old tables of morality, guided like a mysteriously seductive beacon and unfortunately not small part of the German youth, guided it forward into a wholly dark future which must be conquered.

ERICH FROMM
Escape from Freedom

Erich Fromm, like Quigley, blames Hitler on the need of the German people for a strong leader. Fromm, however, is more specific in that he singles out the lower middle class instead of attempting to generalize about all of German society. Furthermore, Fromm attempts to analyze those factors in this aspect of modern society which cause individual men to avoid freedom in favor of a totalitarian system.

THESE ARE the outstanding questions that arise when we look at the human aspect of freedom, the longing for submission, and the lust for power: What is freedom as a human experience? Is the desire for freedom something inherent in human nature? Is it an identical experience regardless of what kind of culture a person lives in, or is it something different according to the degree of individualism reached in a particular society? Is freedom only the absence of external pressure or is it also the presence of something—and if so, of what? What are the social and economic factors in society that make for the striving for freedom? Can freedom become a burden, too heavy for man to bear, something he tries to escape from? Why then is it that freedom is for many a cherished goal and for others a threat?

Is there not also, perhaps, besides an innate desire for freedom, an instinctive wish for submission? If there is not, how can we account for the attraction which submission to a leader has for so many today? Is submission always to an overt authority, or is there also submission to internalized authorities, such as duty or conscience, to inner compulsions or to anonymous authorities like public opinion? Is there a hidden satisfaction in submitting, and what is its essence? . . .

* * *

In our opinion none of these explanations which emphasize political and economic factors to the exclusion of psychological ones—or vice versa—is correct. Nazism is a psychological problem, but the psychological factors themselves have to be understood as being molded by socio-economic factors; Nazism is an economic and political problem, but the hold it has over a whole people has to be understood on psychological grounds. . . .

Members of the older generation among this class [lower middle class] formed the more passive mass basis; their sons and daughters were the more active fighters. For them the Nazi ideology—its spirit of blind obedience to a leader and of hatred against racial and political minorities, its craving for conquest and domination, its exaltation of the German people and the "Nordic Race"—had a tremendous emotional appeal, and it was this appeal which won them over and made them into ardent believers in and fighters for the Nazi cause. The answer to the question why the Nazi ideology was so appealing to the lower middle class has to be sought for in the social character of the lower middle class. Their social character was markedly different from that of the working class, of the higher strata of the middle class, and of the nobility before the war of 1914. As a matter of fact, certain features were characteristic for this part of the middle class throughout its history: their love of the strong, hatred of the weak, their pettiness, hostility, thriftiness with feelings as well as with money, and essentially their asceticism. Their outlook on life was narrow, they suspected and hated the stranger, and they were curious and envious of their acquaintances, rationalizing their envy as moral indignation; their whole life was based on the principle of scarcity—economically as well as psychologically.

To say that the social character of the lower middle class differed from that of the working class does not imply that this character structure was not present in the working class also. But it was *typical* for the lower middle class, while only a minority of the working class exhibited the same character structure in a similarly clear-cut fashion; the one or the other trait, however, in a less intense form, like enhanced respect of authority or thrift, was to be found in most members of the working class too. On the other hand it seems that a great part of the white-collar workers—probably the majority—more closely resembled the character structure of the manual workers (especially those in big factories) than that of the "old middle class," which did not participate in the rise of monopolistic capitalism but was essentially threatened by it.

Although it is true that the social character of the lower middle class had been the same long before the war of 1914, it is also true that the events after the war intensified the very traits to which the Nazi ideology had its strong appeal: its craving for submission and its lust for power.

In the period before the German Revolution of 1918, the economic position of the lower strata of the old middle class, the small independent businessman and artisan, was already on the decline; but it was not desperate and there were a number of factors which made for its stability.

The authority of the monarchy was undisputed, and by leaning on it and identifying with it the member of the lower middle class acquired a feeling of security and narcissistic pride. Also, the authority of religion and traditional morality was still firmly rooted. The family was still unshaken and a safe refuge in a hostile world. The individual felt that he belonged to a stable social and cultural system in which he had his definite place. His submission and loyalty to existing authorities were a satisfactory solution to his masochistic strivings; yet he did not go to the extreme of self-surrender and he retained a sense of the importance of his own personality. What he was lacking in security and aggressiveness as an individual, he was compensated for by the strength of the authorities to whom he submitted himself. In brief his economic position was still solid enough to give him a feeling of self-pride and of relative security, and the authorities on whom he leaned were strong enough to give him the additional security which his own individual position could not provide.

The postwar period changed this situation considerably. In the first place, the economic decline of the old middle class went at a faster pace; this decline was accelerated by the inflation, culminating in 1923, which wiped out almost completely the savings of many years' work.

While the years between 1924 and 1928 brought economic improvement and new hopes to the lower middle class, these gains were wiped out by the depression after 1929. As in the period of inflation, the middle class, squeezed in between the workers and the upper classes, was the most defenseless group and therefore the hardest hit.

But besides these economic factors there were psychological considerations that aggravated the situation. The defeat in war and the downfall of the monarchy was one. While the monarchy and the state had been the solid rock on which, psychologically speaking, the petty bourgeois had built his existence, their failure and defeat shattered the basis of his own life. If the Kaiser could be publicly ridiculed, if officers could be attacked, if the state had to change its form and to accept "red agitators" as cabinet ministers and a saddlemaker as president, what could the little man put his trust in? He had identified himself in his subaltern manner with all these institutions; now, since they had gone, where was he to go?

The inflation, too, played both an economic and a psychological role. It was a deadly blow against the principle of thrift as well as against the authority of the state. If the savings of many years, for which one had sacrificed so many little pleasures, could be lost through no fault of one's own, what was the point in saving anyway? If the state could break its promises printed on its bank notes and loans, whose promises could one trust any longer?

It was not only the economic position of the lower middle class that declined more rapidly after the war, but its social prestige as well. Before the war one could feel himself as something better than a worker. After the revolution the social prestige of the working class rose considerably and in consequence the prestige of the lower middle class fell in relative terms. There was nobody to look down upon any more, a privilege that had always been one of the strongest assets in the life of small shopkeepers and their like.

In addition to these factors the last stronghold of middle-class security had been shattered too: the family. The postwar development, in Germany perhaps more than in other countries, had shaken the authority of the father and the old middle-class morality. The younger generation acted as they pleased and cared no longer whether their actions were approved by their parents or not.

The reasons for this development are too manifold and complex to discuss here in detail. I shall mention only a few. The decline of the old social symbols of authority like monarchy and state affected the role of the individual authorities, the parents. If these authorities, which the younger generation had been taught by the parents to respect, proved to be weak, then the parents lost prestige and authority too. Another factor was that, under the changed conditions, especially the inflation, the older generation was bewildered and puzzled and much less adapted to the new conditions than the smarter, younger generation. Thus the younger generation felt superior to their elders and could not take them, and their teachings, quite seriously any more. Furthermore, the economic decline of the middle class deprived the parents of their economic roles as backers of the economic future of their children.

The older generation of the lower middle class grew more bitter and resentful, but in a passive way; the younger generation was driving for action. Its economic position was aggravated by the fact that the basis for an independent economic existence, such as their parents had had, was lost; the professional market was saturated, and the chances of making a living as a physician or lawyer were slight. Those who had fought in the war felt that they had a claim for a better deal than they were actually getting. Especially the many young officers, who for years had been accustomed to command and to exercise power quite naturally, could not reconcile themselves to becoming clerks or traveling salesmen.

The increasing social frustration led to a projection which became an important source for National Socialism: instead of being aware of the economic and social fate of the old middle class, its members consciously thought of their fate in terms of the nation. The national defeat and the Treaty of Versailles became the symbols to which the actual frustration—the social one—was shifted.

It has often been said that the treatment of Germany by the victors in 1918 was one of the chief reasons for the rise of Nazism. This statement needs qualification. The majority of the Germans felt that the peace treaty was unjust; but while the middle class reacted with intense bitterness, there was much less bitterness at the Versailles Treaty among the working class. They had been opposed to the old regime and the loss of the war meant for them defeat of that regime. They felt that they had fought bravely and that they had no reason to be ashamed of themselves. On the other hand the victory of the revolution which had only been possible by the defeat of the monarchy had brought them economic, political, and human gains. The resentment against Versailles had its basis in the lower middle class; the nationalistic resentment was a rationalization, projecting social inferiority to national inferiority.

This projection is quite apparent in Hitler's personal development. He was the typical representative of the lower middle class, a nobody with no chances or future. He felt very intensely the role of being an outcast. He often speaks in *Mein Kampf* of himself as the "nobody," the "unknown man" he was in his youth. But although this was due essentially to his own social position, he could rationalize it in national symbols. Being born outside of the Reich he felt excluded not so much socially as nationally, and the great German Reich to which all her sons could return became for him the symbol of social prestige and security.

HANS KOHN
The Tragic Character of German History

Hans Kohn in *The Mind of Germany* reflects a view similar to that of Meinecke. Kohn contends that Germany never developed liberal-humanitarian ideas from the Enlightenment to check Hitler as England and France did. Instead, Germany ended up with a modern technological society placed on a pre-modern social and intellectual foundation.

ON OCTOBER 29, 1268, Konradin, the last of the Hohenstaufen, Germany's most ambitious medieval dynasty, mounted a scaffold in the market place of Naples and was put to death. He was then in his seventeenth year. With him the splendor of German imperial grandeur that had dazzled Western Christendom and the Levant for a century ended in tragedy. The reign of the Hohenstaufen was followed by the great interregnum in Germany, the *schreckliche kaiserlose Zeit,* the terrible era without an emperor, as the Germans called it, during which the empire disintegrated, torn by centrifugal forces at a time when the other peoples of Western Christendom, with the exception of Italy, began to consolidate into modern territorial nations. This catastrophe came quite suddenly; only one hundred years before Konradin's birth his great-great-grandfather Frederick Barbarossa had raised German prestige to unprecedented heights.

The memory of Barbarossa's power fascinated the Germans for many centuries after he died leading a crusade in the Near East. A legend originally involving his grandson Frederick II was soon transferred to Barbarossa; it portrayed him asleep deep down inside a mountain—the Untersberg near Salzburg or the Kyffhäuser in Thuringia. But even asleep the hidden emperor remained the guardian of his nation's destiny. If Germany were ever in need of a savior he would be awakened by the ravens encircling his mountain top; he would then rise and lead Germany from defeat and despair to the glory of a new golden age. Compared with this certainty of salvation the actual events of German history and the realities of the world outside were pale indeed; deep down in their hearts the

Germans felt that their true ruler, Germany's *heimliche Kaiser,* was ever ready to come to her rescue. Under the spell of such legends Germans were sometimes in danger of losing sight of political realities and of abandoning themselves to wistful dreams. These overreaching ambitions of the thirteenth century left their mark upon German history: they prevented the consolidation of a rationally circumscribed German political order. When, in the Age of Nationalism, the attempt was made to create German national unity in a modern state the heritage of the Middle Ages was revived: nationalism fused with the consciousness of the imperial mission and with a feeling of superiority of the imperial people, the *Reich.* Modern western science and technology penetrated the new Reich and rapidly transformed it into a nation with the most up-to-date equipment. Yet the social and intellectual substructure remained unchanged: its preservation was even regarded as a mark of true German strength. As a result the tragic story of the Middle Ages repeated itself—great efforts and great achievements ended in an unexpected collapse.

The center of this new Reich was no longer Swabia, the southwestern part of Germany, the home of the Hohenstaufen. The center shifted from western and southern Germany, which from Roman times had been an integral part of the western world, to the lands beyond the Elbe, which in their social and political structure had not followed the development of modern Europe. There Prussia, a small, poor, and backward country on the eastern border of Germany, in many ways culturally and ethnically the least "German" part of the many Germanies of the period, was transformed through the exemplary will power and spartan devotion of Frederick the Great's subjects into a powerful militarized state. But in 1806, only twenty years after the death of its soldier-king, the military might of Prussia ignominiously collapsed. The intercession of the Russian Tsar with Napoleon, at that time, saved Prussia from complete extinction. In ten years, however, a highly intelligent and relentless concentration of all the nation's resources succeeded beyond all expectations in rebuilding Prussian power. Reforms were instituted affecting the political and legal structure of the nation.

Resented by most eighteenth century German intellectuals for its militarism, Prussia became, as a result of these reforms, a center for those who agitated for a strong German nation-state. The great historian Johann Gustav Droysen, then teaching at the University of Kiel, stressed, in a memorandum of April 26, 1848, Germany's need of a "powerful ruling house." He was convinced that only Prussia could fill the need by offering her *Machtorganisation,* her power concentration, especially her military and financial system, as a model for the whole of Germany."To the Hohenzollern," Droysen concluded, "belongs the place which has been empty since the days of the Hohenstaufen."

Droysen's wish came true. Bismarck, Prime Minister for twenty-eight years, made Prussia the brain and heart of modern Germany. It has often been said that in this process Prussia, which covered about three-fourths of the imperial territory, was only partly Germanized whereas the large parts of Germany which had fallen under Prussian leadership became Prussianized. Yet this Prussianization was hardly a blessing for Germany. Her temporary security was based upon Bismarck's moderation in foreign policy. Catastrophe quickly overtook Germany, and with her Europe, when Bismarck's successors, the victims of a psychological dynamism created by the great Chancellor himself, abandoned his moderation for aspirations as vague as those of any Hohenstaufen.

For the rapid deterioration of post-Bismarckian German statesmanship Bismarck himself was responsible. In his foreign policy after 1871 he rarely used the crude and violent methods which characterized his actions before the moment when Prussia reached, in his opinion, the saturation point of her or his territorial aspirations; after that, however, he applied this aggressive manner even more openly in his domestic policy. His cynical contempt for parliamentary liberalism and his insistence on authoritarian leadership kept the German middle class from active participation in government and precluded its growth to political maturity and responsible thinking. Nor did he inspire confidence in German intentions abroad.

The situation grew worse after the young Emperor William II dismissed Bismarck in 1890. The Emperor, who wished to be his own chancellor, exhibited Bismarck's ideological and temperamental shortcomings to a heightened degree without the old man's strength and judgment. Year by year, the world grew more and more concerned.

In 1912 Romain Rolland, a fervent European pacifist and a sharp critic of French nationalism who was wholly free of anti-German sentiment, conveyed in his novel *Jean-Christophe* the deep misgivings about Germany which by then were felt by even the most dispassionate observers of the European scene. His hero, a German musician who had lived most of his mature life in France and Italy, stressed Germany's responsibility for a Europe which Bismarck's victory over France at Sedan in 1870 had transformed into a military camp seething with mutual suspicions:

> Although [Jean-Christophe] had spent a few months in Germany and returned there from time to time to conduct performances of his works, he did not settle there. He found too many things there which hurt him. They were not peculiar to Germany; he found them elsewhere too. But a man expects more of his own country than of any other, and he suffers more from its foibles. It was true too, that Germany was bearing the greatest burden of the sins of Europe. The victor incurs the responsibility of his victory, a debt toward the vanquished: tacitly the victor is pledged to march in front of them to show the way. The conquests of Louis XIV gave Europe the splendor of French reason. What light has the Germany of Sedan given to the world? The glitter of bayonets, thought without wings, action without generosity, brutal realism, which has not even the excuse of being the realism of healthy men; force and interest; Mars turned traveling salesman. Forty years ago (1871) Europe was led astray into the night and the terrors of the night. The sun was hidden beneath the conqueror's helmet. If the vanquished can claim only pity mingled with contempt, what shall be given to the victor who has done this thing?

At the beginning of the twentieth century Germany's neighbors feared her vague aspirations and her threatening gestures. As in the time of the Hohenstaufen, the German *Reich* in 1914 entered a gigantic struggle without a true estimate of its real strength and without understanding the changing realities of Europe and of the world. As a result, only twenty years after Bismarck's death, the mighty empire which he had established through war and which seemed so impregnable in its armed might, economic strength, and advanced scholarship foundered in defeat. The warning against the *hubris* of power which the defeat of 1918 should have carried remained unheeded by the Germans. On the contrary, in an effort surpassing all those of the past, and with all the deep earnestness of their dedicated discipline and feeling of superiority, the Germans rallied around a man who in his appeal to many of their folk myths and resentments appeared to them as the *heimliche Kaiser*, risen from the depth in Germany's hour of direst need to waken her and lead her to the glorious fulfillment of her mission. But this third attempt, which promised to last a thousand years, ended in an unprecedented catastrophe in which the last vestiges of the Bismarckian Reich and of Prussia itself disappeared.

From the Hohenstaufen to the Hohenzollern, Germany has written some truly tragic pages in the history of Europe. Perhaps for this reason Germans have claimed to feel the tragic character of history more strongly and to meditate more intensely about it than do others. This pessimistic attitude toward history divides the Germans from the English-speaking peoples and has made mutual understanding in the realm of political thought difficult indeed. The Germans easily succumb to the strange fascination which words such as *Schicksal* (fate) or *Verhängnis* (doom) exercise upon them. These are both words which are used as a matter of course in their scholarly writings and among the general public. They convey an untranslatable overtone of inevitability. They endow many Germans with the certainty of understanding the course of history in a deeper way than the more superficial peoples of the West. In this higher spirituality these Germans found a compensation for Germany's allegedly undeserved national misfortunes.

The question whether German history has formed the German character or whether the character of the Germans has influenced the course of their history has been widely discussed in recent years. Many observers asked themselves whether National Socialism was a natural outcome of German intellectual and political development, or whether Hitlerism—as some Germans maintained—was alien to the German character and traditions and imposed upon Germany by events and influences from without. Did National Socialism represent the "organic" culmination of German history or a monstrous deviation from it? Some German historians went so far in their attempt to vindicate recent German history as to argue that National Socialism was only the German manifestation of a general European movement, characteristic of the age of the rising masses, in which the true Germany, represented by the educated upper class, was swept away by the mounting tide of "democracy." Did not the essential elements of National Socialism originate abroad, they asked: the totalitarian state in Russia, fascism in Italy, the racial theory in France? Was not genuine German "idealism" drowned in the onrush of industrial technology and economic materialism which had come from the West and which alone had rendered Hitler's mass-demagogy possible? Though these attempts to burden the West and modern society with the responsibility for Germany's

National Socialism contain, as does every theory, an element of truth, they are fundamentally mistaken; worse, however, they render a disservice to Germany, for they overlook the specific German intellectual and political heritage which made the Germans acclaim Hitler's rise to power. Germany did not succumb to Hitler because she had become part of modern western society; she succumbed because this modern society had been imposed on pre-modern social and intellectual foundations which were proudly retained.

National Socialism was as little the natural or logical outcome of German history as Leninism was of Russian history. There is no inevitability in history. Before 1914 there was good hope that the liberal and western trends in Germany and in Russia might slowly grow in strength and transform the social structure, political thought, and institutions of the two nations. Without the catastrophe of the First World War, without the ensuing economic chaos, and probably without the decisive personalities of Lenin and Hitler, neither Bolshevism nor National Socialism would have come to power. But the recognition of these historical circumstances does not imply that the success of the extremist movements was accidental or primarily due to external factors. Communism and National Socialism were made possible by the historical and political traditions of the two nations involved—not by what they had in common with the West but by what separated their intellectual and social development from that of the West.

Hitler's claim to represent the true interests of the German people could find credence because he appealed to sentiments deeply rooted both in the educated classes and in the people. His was not the only country in which such sentiments existed, but in Germany they were not held in check by the liberal-humanitarian considerations Western Europe inherited from the Enlightenment. Hitler was especially successful in appealing to what the Germans regarded as deep and idealistic in their past and their minds. He knew that the best way to lead Germans was by involving a metaphysical system that would confer on their political actions and on their national desires the consecration of history and divine guidance. Thus National Socialism—in spite of its distortions—could pretend to lead a crusade to realize Germany's age-old longings and her sense of historical mission. Once National Socialism had assumed control its claims were supported by the German habit of trusting those in authority. This century-old

disposition had been powerfully reinforced by Germany's unification through Bismarck's authoritarian methods and Prussia's
military might. For Hitler was the heir—even if illegitimate— of
German romantic myth and of Prussian militarist efficiency. His was
a vulgarized form of the militarism which, to quote a contemporary
German scholar, "made everything instrumental to the demands of
dark, subconscious urges." National Socialism succeeded among
many Germans in removing the rational and moral restraints imposed by "alien" Christianity and "alien" liberal western thought.

The Germans have been fascinated by the concepts of *Geist,* a
term best translated as spiritual depth, and *Macht,* authoritarian
power. In the eighteenth century German intellectuals and the
German people underrated the importance of power and overrated
purity of spirit. They seemed to the western world an idyllic
apolitical people of poets and thinkers. This attitude changed in the
nineteenth century. From one extreme the Germans moved to
another. They remained fundamentally apolitical, animated by
haughty contempt for politics, but they became a dynamic nation
whose will centered upon power and the power-state. From the life
of the spirit, which characterized the period from 1740 to 1814, they
turned to the pursuit of power. Having lived so long outside of
active participation in political history, educated Germans tended to
overstress the concepts of state and power. They rejected the
rational and critical control of *Macht* by *Geist;* instead, under the
pretext of a synthesis of spirit and power, they idealized the
power-state and transformed it from an instrument of the spirit into
its embodiment. Their leading thinkers of the early nineteenth
century—Fichte, Hegel, and Marx—raised the nation, the state, and
the economy to supreme concepts, regarded history with its con-
flicts as the unfolding of an ultimate and self-justifying reality, and
distorted political processes to fit a semireligious utopianism. Under
the influence of these and similar thinkers German thought after
1812 consciously deviated from the main lines of western development.

Throughout history, and especially in modern times, many people
everywhere have succumbed to the demonic temptation of power
and of the will-to-power which Nietzsche proclaimed the fundamental life-force. But beginning with their greatest nineteenth
century philosopher, Hegel, and their greatest modern historian,
Ranke, the Germans have often refused to recognize the demonic
character of power; on the contrary, they have surrounded power

with the halo of a philosophy which they extolled for its alleged understanding of history and human nature, an understanding, as they claimed, deeper than the superficial western moralism which to them only masked the power-drive. In the modern West, people distrusted power and feared its abuse; the modern Germans felt an almost religious reverence for power—Ranke regarded it as the manifestation of a spiritual essence—and for its embodiment in the authority of the state. State and power found in later nineteenth century Germany their most popular symbol in the army and the uniform—to partake of them gave even the humblest German a proud feeling of belonging, of belonging to a national whole whose armed power, whose loftiness of ideas, whose sense of discipline and service were without rivals.

In the sixth decade of the nineteenth century, liberalism was in the ascendancy throughout Europe. The whole continent seemed destined to follow the example set by the English model of state and society. This prevailing trend toward liberalism was reversed—in Germany first and in much of the European continent thereafter—when Bismarck, with the enthusiastic acclaim of the German people, forged a new Reich in conscious opposition to liberal democracy. Richard Wagner, the greatest German artist of the period, in most ways quite unlike Bismarck, with equal incisiveness rejected the liberal West. On his grandiose stage he revived primitive native heroes and gods singing of fate and doom and rushing toward their own annihilation through a web of crime and deceit. Neither Bismarck in his statesmanship nor Wagner in his art, neither Germany groping for leadership before 1914, nor Germany over-reaching itself for an even more ambitious goal in 1939, had any generous universal message to carry to other peoples. Other European nations, too, had tried to dominate the scene: all of them—from Catholic Spain under Philip II to Communist Russia under Lenin—thought of mankind as well as of their own nation. They brought a spiritual or social message which inspired millions in other lands. In an exemplary way, seventeenth century England embodied the universal idea of liberty; eighteenth century France that of reason. Among all the great nations Germany alone, when its turn came, had nothing to offer but self-centered power and self-glorification.

II Problems of the Republic

The problems of a newly constituted government are always serious. But the Weimar Republic faced problems matched in the West only by those of the new Russian government in 1917. The Versailles Treaty was dictated as an ultimatum to the new German government. Many of the terms were historically and psychologically unsound. The new constitution itself created additional problems for the embryonic Republic. In a sense the borrowings from England and France were simply grafted onto the existing social, political, and economic power structure. The result was, perhaps inevitably, since Germany had not experienced a genuine revolution, a democratic system run by either non- or anti-democrats.

The still-powerful military caste had no intention of associating itself with responsibility for the problems facing the new government. The judges failed miserably to provide justice. Political parties were narrowly conceived and class-oriented.

Even with these crippling disabilities the Weimar Republic might have survived until it gained prestige and respect had it not had to deal with two great economic crises in a short span of time. The inflation of 1923 almost destroyed the middle class, but the Republic survived and by drastic action stabilized its currency and economy. The effect of the Great Depression, however, coming so soon after the inflation, brought about a polarization of politics. In their search for solutions the people turned left to the Communists, or right to the blandishments of Adolf Hitler and his Nazi party.

Articles 231 and 232 of the Versailles Treaty

Articles 231 and 232 of the Treaty of Versailles stipulated that because Germany was the sole cause of World War I, she must pay the cost of the war. These two articles caused much bitterness and hate in Germany, especially after 1923 when no one in Europe believed that Germany was the sole cause of the war. But Germany still had to pay reparations.

ARTICLE 231.

The Allied and Associated Governments affirm and Germany accepts the responsibility of Germany and her allies for causing all the loss and damage to which the Allied and Associated Governments and their nationals have been subjected as a consequence of the war imposed upon them by the aggression of Germany and her allies.

ARTICLE 232.

The Allied and Associated Governments recognize that the resources of Germany are not adequate, after taking into account permanent diminutions of such resources which will result from other provisions of the present Treaty, to make complete reparation for all such loss and damage.

The Allied and Associated Governments, however, require, and Germany undertakes, that she will make compensation for all damage done to the civilian population of the Allied and Associated Powers and to their property during the period of the belligerency of each as an Allied or Associated Power against Germany by such aggression by land, by sea and from the air, and in general all damage as defined in Annex I hereto.

In accordance with Germany's pledges, already given, as to complete restoration for Belgium, Germany undertakes, in addition to the compensation for damage elsewhere in this Part provided for, as a consequence of the violation of the Treaty of 1839, to make reimbursement of all sums which Belgium has borrowed from the Allied and Associated Governments up to November 11, 1918, together with interest at the rate of five per cent (5%) per annum on such sums. This amount shall be determined by the Reparation

From Allied and Associated Powers (1914-1920), *Treaty with Germany,* June 28, 1919 (Washington: Government Printing Office, 1919), pp. 91–92, 95–96.

Commission, and the German Government undertakes thereupon forthwith to make a special issue of bearer bonds to an equivalent amount payable in marks gold, on May 1, 1926, or, at the option of the German Government, on the 1st of May in any year up to 1926. Subject to the foregoing, the form of such bonds shall be determined by the Reparation Commission. Such bonds shall be handed over to the Reparation Commission, which has authority to take and acknowledge receipt thereof on behalf of Belgium.

ANNEX I.

Compensation may be claimed from Germany under Article 232 above in respect of the total damage under the following categories:

1. Damage to injured persons and to surviving dependents by personal injury to or death of civilians caused by acts of war, including bombardments or other attacks on land, on sea, or from the air, and all the direct consequence thereof, and of all operations of war by the two groups of belligerents wherever arising.

2. Damage caused by Gemany or her allies to civilian victims of acts of cruelty, violence or maltreatment (including injuries to life or health as a consequence of imprisonment, deportation, internment or evacuation, of exposure at sea or of being forced to labour), wherever arising, and to the surviving dependents of such victims.

3. Damage caused by Germany or her allies in their own territory or in occupied or invaded territory to civilian victims of all acts injurious to health or capacity to work, or to honour, as well as to the surviving dependents of such victims.

4. Damage caused by any kind of maltreatment of prisoners of war.

5. As damage caused to the peoples of the Allied and Associated Powers, all pensions and compensation in the nature of pensions to naval and military victims of war (including members of the air force), whether mutilated, wounded, sick or invalided, and to the dependents of such victims, the amount due to the Allied and Associated Governments being calculated for each of them as being the capitalized cost of such pensions and compensation at the date of the coming into force of the present Treaty on the basis of the scales in force in France at such date.

6. The cost of assistance by the Government of the Allied and Associated Powers to prisoners of war and to their families and dependents.

7. Allowances by the Governments of the Allied and Associated Powers to the families and dependents of mobilized persons or persons serving with the forces, the amount due to them for each calendar year in which hostilities occurred being calculated for each Government on the basis of the average scale for such payments in force in France during that year.

8. Damage caused to civilians by being forced by Germany or her allies to labour without just remuneration.

9. Damage in respect of all property wherever situated belonging to any of the Allied or Associated States or their nationals, with the exception of naval and military works or materials, which has been carried off, seized, injured or destroyed by the acts of Germany or her allies on land, on sea or from the air, or damage directly in consequences of hostilities or of any operations of war.

10. Damage in the form of levies, fines and other similar exactions imposed by Germany or her allies upon the civilian population.

MAXIMILIAN MONTGELAS
An Impeachment of the Versailles Verdict

Maximilian Montgelas refutes Article 231 of the Treaty of Versailles. He admonishes the men at Versailles for indicting Germany when they had not seen either their own state records or the records of the belligerent powers. As evidence that Germany was not the sole cause of the war, Montgelas presents the political aims of the great powers as well as their war preparations. In a later section of his book, Montgelas deals with the other points in the Versailles indictment.

WHAT BISMARCK has said as to a terrible war, which would set Europe in flames from Moscow to the Pyrenees, and end in no one knowing why they had fought, came to pass in the second decade of the twentieth century. What could have brought about an international conflict which devastated extensive tracts of land, cut off

---

Reprinted by permission from Maximilian Montgelas, *The Case for the Central Powers, An Impeachment of the Versailles Verdict,* trans. by Contance Vesey (New York: A. A. Knopf, London: George Allen & Unwin, Ltd., 1925), pp. 11-17.

many millions of men in the flower of their youth, and crippled the economic strength of our continent for generations to come?

One answer is that the world war was inevitable, because all the Great Powers, without exception, were saturated with Imperialism, only intent upon extending their power and securing it, by rival armaments on land, at sea, and in the air. War was bound to come, because the Governments had forgotten that peace alone can serve the true interests of nations, and the peoples failed to realize the economic solidarity of their countries.

This, no doubt, may explain some of the underlying causes of the great catastrophe, although to accept the world war as having been inevitable might savour too much of fatalism, and seems to take the influence of leading politicians into too little account. But there is no need to consider here how far such resignation is justifiable. Our object is to enquire into the justice of another answer—the one given at Versailles by accusers who set themselves up at the same time as judges, and this at a time when none of the belligerent Powers' archives had been published in full. Men who had not seen either their adversaries' or their allies' State records, and who carefully preserved strict secrecy as regards their own, maintained in Article 231 of the dictated Peace that the war had been imposed upon them by the aggression of Germany and her allies. And, stripped of its profuse verbiage, the gist of the ultimatum of June 16, 1919, which forced Germany to sign her political and moral death warrant, is simply as follows:

Of all the Powers, Germany was the only one prepared for a great war.

For decades past Germany had systematically prepared for an offensive war of conquest and subjugation, and had deliberately kindled this war in 1914, in order to acquire the upper hand in Europe, and achieve her aims of world supremacy.

The nations who opposed her were only bent on preserving their liberty.

On the many occasions when the world had been divided up in former days, Germany had been left out in the cold, and even in the re-partitions of the last few decades, she had come off very badly. In 1914 the German Empire had a population of sixty-seven million in the mother country, and a colonial population of only twelve million. The German people did not aspire to world supremacy, but only to a modest "place in the sun," an aim which was surely attainable without war, and without injuring the interests of other nations. The colonial agreement with England, which had already been drafted, and which would have done justice to Germany's legitimate and moderate demands, was actually to have been signed in August of the fatal year.

As against this, France, with her population of thirty-nine million, had succeeded, after 1871, in building up a powerful colonial Empire, with fifty-three million coloured subjects, from modest beginnings. That had only been possible thanks to Bismarck's moral and diplomatic support. The security afforded by the first German Chancellor's assurance that Germany would not attack her, no matter how many French troops were sent across the water, enabled the Republic to acquire Tunis, Annam, Tongking, Laos, and valuable territory in West Africa, as well as the island of Madagascar. The last ten years, however, had secured Morocco to the French, who were infringing one treaty after another, and it was in Morocco that the ball was to be set rolling which ended in world war, as will be shown later on.

The British Empire was still more powerful. There were only forty-six million inhabitants of the British Islands, but, of the total population of the world, three hundred and seventy-six million, that is more than one-fifth of its inhabitants, were subjects of His Britannic Majesty. In spite of this, the British Imperialists continued to pursue their aims. The great Cape to Cairo railway was to be constructed in Africa, and overland communication established from thence between West and East, via Palestine, Arabia, and Mesopotamia, to India. At the same time, the ever vigilant British Admiralty were endeavoring to secure still firmer control of the high seas, by acquiring fresh naval bases, and preventing such bases being acquired by opponents of the Triple Entente. Just as England ruled over the seas, and the largest number of peoples of various races and religions, so Russia held sway over the most extensive domains. Her vast territorial possessions formed a concrete whole, but many of the peoples united under the Tsar's rule were of foreign origin.

Even small countries like Holland and Belgium owned more extensive and more thickly populated colonies than Germany.

The second charge against Germany, namely that she aspired to "supremacy in Europe," can equally be refuted. Germany did not want a foot of territory in Europe over and above what she had acquired in 1871. The island of Heligoland, which had been offered by England even earlier, was made over to her by friendly agreement in 1890, in return for extensive renunciation of territory in Africa.

It was otherwise in France and Russia. The belief that, after 1871, France was only bent on recovering Alsace and Lorraine, has proved to have been mistaken. We know now, from the reports of the French Ambassador, Baron Courcel, that, even at the end of 1884, consequently at a time when Germany went particularly far towards meeting the French wishes, leading French politicians still refused to accept the treaties of 1815 as final, and wanted to recover the German Saar district, which, for some inconceivable reasons, had been left to France by the Peace of 1814. Delcasse's reports on what he described as the "remarkable" extension of the Franco-Russian alliance he had achieved in the summer of 1899, revealed a third aim, in addition to Alsace-Lorraine and the Saar: in case of the Habsburg Empire breaking up, the union of German-Austria with the great mother country was to be prevented, if necessary by force of arms. Following upon that, it will be seen how Delcasse, Poincare's right hand, discussed France's territorial aims in Europe with Sazonov in 1913, a year and a half before the outbreak of war. The Sedan defeat had no more succeeded in preventing France from trying to push her frontiers permanently further east than the defeat of Waterloo.

Russia too no longer fixed her attention exclusively on Asiatic territory. . . . It need only be said here that, at the beginning of 1914, St. Petersburg had adopted the view that the domination of the Bosphorus and Dardanelles, to which Russia aspired, could only be achieved "within the framework of a European war."

Whilst the Triple Entente Powers were making these far-reaching plans, and Germany aspired to a place in the sun, Austria's sole aim was the maintenance of the *status quo*. Although this may be said to have been an unjustifiable anachronism, in view of the fact that there were a certain number of South Slavs who wished for the erection of a Greater-Serbian State, no serious politician can ever have thought of crediting Austria-Hungary with any aspirations to world power, or any wish to dominate Europe.

Thus it will be seen that neither Berlin nor Vienna had aims which could only be realized through a sea of blood and tears. Even the English Imperialists' ambitious schemes might indeed have been accomplished without a European war, for they were only directed against defenseless nations in other parts of the world. On the other hand, the territorial ambitions of France, Russia, and the nations under Russia's protection, were only attainable on the battlefields of Europe.

The third charge made by the ultimatum is that Germany had been preparing for a war of aggression for many decades past. Whoever drew up the indictment—it is said to have been an Englishman— forgot that, just ten years before the catastrophe, Great Britain had been most anxious to form an alliance with Germany, an alliance directed against both France and Russia, later on her allies.

To refute this charge, it is hardly necessary to go back to Bismarck's day. The publication of State Papers by the German Foreign Office, including a number of strictly confidential memoranda and written instructions, has revealed the first German Chancellor's most secret aims and intentions to the whole world, which has been amazed to find how very much his policy had been a policy of peace ever since the foundation of the Empire. It was not only a policy of peace for Germany, but for the whole of Europe, based, not on any Pacifist theories, but on practical recognition that this alone could serve the true interests of both Empire and people. . . .

There is no doubt that, after Bismarck's time, Germany's policy was directed by a far less sure hand. Fault may well be found with a great deal in the methods of this period of the Wilhelminic epoch. Many a diplomatic move was made, which would never have been sanctioned by such an excellent pilot as the first Chancellor. The unnecessary prominence given to the person of the Monarch, provocative speeches, bellicose talk, and theatrical gestures, all combined to give malicious people in other countries ample ground for carrying on inflammatory propaganda, while, at the same time, it did not the least alarm Germany's opponents, for they well knew that these demonstrations were not backed by any strength of purpose. According to evidence given on oath by men who had gone through the many thousand volumes of Foreign Office Papers, not one of them contains a single document showing any sign of belligerent intentions. It must further be evident to anyone who reflects at all, that if Germany had wished to embark on a war of aggression, or even only on a preventive war, it would have been brought about at a time when the political and military position was favourable. . . .

Article 48 of the Weimar Constitution

Article 48 of the Weimar Constitution allowed the Republic's President to suspend certain of the constitutional guarantees of Fundamental Rights in a time of national emergency. The decision whether a given situation constituted such an emergency was left entirely to the discretion of the President,who was thus given enormous authoritarian powers.

ARTICLE 48

If any state does not fulfill the duties imposed upon it by the Constitution or the laws of the Reich, the Reich President may enforce such duties with the aid of the armed forces.

In the event that the public order and security are seriously disturbed or endangered, the Reich President may take the measures necessary for their restoration, intervening, if necessary, with the aid of the armed forces. For this purpose he may temporarily abrogate, wholly or in part, the fundamental principles laid down in Articles 114, 115, 117, 118, 123, 124, and 153.

The Reich President must, without delay, inform the Reichstag of all measures taken under Paragraph 1 or Paragraph 2 of this Article. These measures taken may be rescinded on demand of the Reichstag. . . .

ARTICLE 114

Personal liberty is inviolable. Curtailment or deprivation of personal liberty by a public authority is permissible only by authority of law.

Persons who have been deprived of their liberty must be informed at the latest on the following day by whose authority and for what reasons they have been held. They shall receive the opportunity without delay of submitting objections to their deprivation of liberty.

ARTICLE 115

The house of every German is his sanctuary and is inviolable. Exceptions are permitted only by authority of law. . . .

From *The Weimar Republic* by Louis L. Snyder, Copyright © 1966, by Louis L. Snyder, by permission of Van Nostrand Reinhold Company.

ARTICLE 117

The secrecy of letters and all postal, telegraph, and telephone communications is inviolable. Exceptions are inadmissible except by national law.

ARTICLE 118

Every German has the right, within the limits of the general laws, to express his opinion freely by word, in writing, in print, in picture form, or in any other way. . . . Censorship is forbidden. . . .

ARTICLE 123

All Germans have the right to assemble peacefully and unarmed without giving notice and without special permission. . . .

ARTICLE 124

All Germans have the right to form associations and societies for purposes not contrary to the criminal law. . . .

ARTICLE 153

The right of private property is guaranteed by the Constitution. . . . Expropriation of property may take place . . . by due process of law. . . .

RUPERT EMERSON
Sovereignty in the Republic

Rupert Emerson in *State and Sovereignty in Modern Germany* argues that the Weimar Constitution established a state to manage the affairs of the German people, but not to impose the will of an authoritarian government on the people. Emerson's contention is a very definite contrast to the realities of Articles 47 and 48, which allowed for an authoritarian government to exist. The reader must realize, however, that Emerson's book was written in 1928, before the Republic was threatened by the economic consequences of the 1929 Wall Street Crash.

To POLITICAL THEORY in general the German Revolution made one important contribution, but to the theory of sovereignty in particular it added virtually nothing. The outstanding political achievement of the Revolution was the transformation of monarchial sovereignty into popular sovereignty: every other point was debatable, but there was no one to dispute that sovereignty had passed definitely from the crowned heads of Germany to the German people. On the ninth of November, 1918, Prince Max of Baden, the last imperial chancellor, announced prematurely that "the Kaiser and King has decided to abdicate," and on the same day Ebert and Scheidemann proclaimed the German Republic in Berlin: "the new government will be a people's government." Not until the twenty-eighth did there come the official word from the former Kaiser: "I herewith renounce for all time all rights to the crown of Prussia and the rights connected therewith, to the imperial crown." In the interval every other throne in Germany had fallen, and the people were in full command of their own destinies.

The transition to popular sovereignty did not, however, in itself serve to work any fundamental change in the theory of sovereignty. The possibilities of this form had been too widely explored both in Germany and elsewhere to allow new discoveries to be made in relation to it. Furthermore, the theory of popular sovereignty had never seriously been excluded in Germany even though the discussion of it had remained largely academic, due in part to the actual

From Rupert Emerson, *State and Sovereignty in Modern Germany* (New Haven: Yale University Press, 1928), pp. 212, 215-217, 232, 234.

political situation and in larger part to the approval generally felt in Germany for the principle of monarchy. . . . The formal principle of sovereignty played virtually no part in all the discussion that raged around the framing of the new Constitution. There was none to plead for anarchy and none who bothered to attack the principle that the "State" should be "sovereign." Furthermore, the monarchical principle had been eliminated from practical policies for the time being: the few voices that were raised in its favor in the two or three years following the revolution were apologetic and ready to admit that the democracy which they distrusted was the order of the day. The rather conservative-minded Democrats, while protesting that they had been no opponents of monarchy, recognized that "one foundation-stone which we cannot fit into the new structure is monarchy. . . . When the tree is lying on the ground after having been uprooted, it is impossible to set it up again." There was general agreement with the view expressed by Hugo Preuss that even if the pendulum should swing back, the classical monarchical principle would be shattered, and the new monarchy would have to be founded explicitly on popular consent.

Here lay the essential difference between the problems of 1848 and 1919: excluding the issue of federalism in each case, the one centered about monarchy vs. democracy, the other about Social Democracy vs. bolshevism. The year 1848 was essentially concerned with the freedom of the individual, with the abolition of individual or class political privileges, and with the Bill of Rights which so largely contributed to its lack of success. In 1919, as Hermann Oncken noted, "the center of gravity of the movement has shifted from the political to the social, and instead of the form of the State the form of society will be the final goal of the struggles of the future." Thus where sovereignty—of monarch or of people—played a great part in the *Paulskirche,* it dropped almost out of sight at Weimar and in the events preceding Weimar.

It has been said by one of the tried leaders of Social Democracy in Germany that the essential issue of the Revolution was the conflict between two fundamentally different conceptions of socialism and social evolution. The sovereignty of the people had come, and with it, as a necessary consequence, democracy. But "democracy" had two extreme meanings and many shades of those two in between: Was democracy to be the rule of the whole people through the ballot box and the parliament, or was it to be democracy on the Russian model, the democracy of the proletariat? It was on this line that the

Revolution was fought. The majority of the Socialists and the parties on the right defended the principle that the whole people must determine its own destinies and shoulder its own responsibilities: as one Socialist speaker said, no more socialism shall be imposed than the people themselves freely want. To this the groups on the left replied that the vanguard of the proletariat must safeguard the fruits of the Revolution for the proletariat and crush out the swift-growing weeds of capitalism which would again overwhelm the workers if substantial economic and social despotism were allowed to coexist with formal political freedom. . . .

* * *

From one standpoint there could be no doubt of the sovereignty of the people. The Constitution itself in its first article proclaimed not only that "the German Reich is a republic," but as well that "the political power emanates from the people," and there was a general tendency even among the critical to accept this statement of fact as indicating that sovereignty must be lodged at the source from which political power is derived. In other words, it was natural to conclude that the people were sovereign and the exercise of their sovereignty was entrusted for the most part to the Reichstag; but this view was not allowed to go unchallenged.

It was undeniable that popular sovereignty expressed itself in the elections to the presidency and to the Reichstag and further in the several provisions for popular votes and referendums. "Nevertheless," insisted one critic, "the highest power does not really rest with the people, since the Constitution can be changed and all the constitutional rights of the people set aside without the people being able to protect itself. The so-called obligatory constitutional referendum is lacking. And even inside the Constitution the ordering of a referendum against an enactment of the Reichstag has been made exceptionally difficult politically in most cases, because the order for a referendum must be countersigned; but the chancellor and the ministers of the Reich require the confidence of the Reichstag. . . .

Under the Weimar Constitution the president is popularly elected and is equipped with numerous opportunities to appeal to the people against the Reichstag, but these appeals are always subject to the counter-signature of the chancellor or ministers. The president cannot, however, be said to rival the power of the Reichstag in himself since, broadly speaking, his only power is that of submitting matters to the people for decision. . . .

Hugo Preuss himself, always dubious of any strict concept of sovereignty, argues that although the new Constitution puts the Reichstag at the center of the life of the State, this in no way signifies unlimited autocratic sovereignty of Parliament. On the contrary, the principle of the constitutional State, established on the basis of law, required the coexistence of several supreme organs of the State between which parliamentary government forms the elastic link; and it requires the control of independent courts which can determine the legality of all private and public acts. A very similar view was taken by Otto Meissner, who saw the Reichstag as the predominant and most important organ of popular sovereignty and as chief bearer of the power of the Reich, but recognized the president as also a bearer of that power through his popular election and his independence of the Reichstag.

Before passing to federalism there remains one question which it is by no means simple to answer. Did the German idea of the State undergo a change as a result of the Revolution and the new Constitution? Did the *Obrigkeitsstaat* maintain its predominancy, or did popular sovereignty bring with it the idea of the *Volksstaat* for which Preuss had pleaded? Evidence in quantities can be produced to support either view, but in general there is little doubt that the State has come to be regarded rather as the political organization of the people for the management of their own affairs, than as a political organization imposed on the people for the carrying out of the will of an authoritarian government. With the passing of monarchy the symbol of the State as sovereign Person standing high above the people was removed. The philosophic jurist had on the whole ignored the conception of the State as power exercised from above and embodied in the head of the State. The Revolution had thrown power into the hands of the people, and the Constitution had been framed by the directly elected representatives of the people. In addition, all, as in the title page of Hobbes, had formed part of the body of the Leviathan throughout the cruel years of the War. The post-war and post-Revolution State in Germany was a State founded on the sacrifices of every German citizen and rebuilt through the labor of the people.

PAUL VON HINDENBURG
The Stab-in-the-Back Myth

The following selection is a translation of Field Marshal Paul von Hindenburg's testimony at the end of the war. Hindenburg was Supreme High Commander of the German army, and in 1925 was elected President of the Weimar Republic. The general blamed the civilian leadership for the loss of the war, the same leaders that Hindenburg worked with later as President of the Republic. It was this statement which popularized the myth of the stab-in-the-back.

WHEN WE were appointed to the Supreme High Command of the Army the World War had been going on for two years. Events which occurred after the 29th of August, 1916, must not be judged except in connection with those which preceded this date.

The war between Germany and Austria-Hungary, on the one hand, and Russia, France and Serbia and, shortly thereafter, Belgium, England and Japan, on the other, had increased in extent. In 1915, Italy, and in 1916, Roumania, entered the conflict on the side of our enemies. With this, the war ceased to have any further counterpart in history. Territory covered approached the limits of the gigantic, the masses of armed men reached numbers hitherto unconceived, and the technical feature attained a predominating significance. War and world economics were intertwined to an extent which had never existed heretofore. The comparative numbers for fighting purposes, of machines and ammunition, and of economic resources had been, and this had been true from the very beginning, as unfavorable as possible for us. At no time were the intangible elements of war so difficult to sustain, such as the morale of the troops and the requirements made upon central and local leadership; and, in a word, never was the minority given so tremendous a burden to bear, as in the course of this war. The Supreme High Command of the Army had to meet the calls of this fundamental characteristic of the war; it was upon the meeting of its requirements that our ceaseless endeavors were centered. Upborne

From *Official German Documents Relating to the World War,* trans. under the supervision of the Carnegie Endowment for International Peace Division of International Law (2 vols; New York: Oxford University Press, 1923), II, 851-855.

by the love of our country, we had but one purpose; to keep the German Empire and the German people, as far as human endeavor and military means could do so, safe from harm, and to guide it by military methods to the point of obtaining a satisfactory peace. In order to carry out this tremendous task, undertaken under these tremendous difficulties, we were bound to maintain the rock-ribbed will to conquer. But this will to conquer was inextricably bound up in the assurance that we were in the right. And with all this, we were well aware that we were bound to succumb in the unequal conflict unless the combined forces of the people at home were directed toward victory on the field of battle, and unless the morale of the Army were continuously fed from home. The will to conquer, of course, did not manifest itself to us as a matter of a purely personal determination, but as an expression of the will of the people. If we had not had this will to conquer, or had not naturally assumed that it existed in the hearts of the people, we would not have undertaken our difficult duties. A general who is not willing to fight in order to gain victory for his country should take over no command, or, if he does so, only with the simultaneous duty of capitulating. No such duty as this was imposed upon us. If it had been, we should have refused to accept the Supreme High Command of the Army.

The German General Staff is based upon the teachings of the great war philosopher Clausewitz. Accordingly, we look upon war as nothing but the continuation of politics, by dint of other means than those of statesmanship, that is, by force of arms. Our peace policy had failed. We desired no war, and yet came to be faced with the greatest—

The CHAIRMAN: Just a minute! This is an expression of opinion, and I should like to call attention to the fact that expressions of opinion are to be eliminated from the testimony of the witnesses. So I protest against this sentence.

Witness V. HINDENBURG: —with the greatest, the most difficult, and the bitterest that history has ever known. How it came to be such, is a matter which history must decide. But I know one thing with absolute certainty: The German people did not want the war, the German Emperor did not want the war, the Government did not want the war, and certainly the General Staff did not want it, for the Staff knew better than anyone else what a terrifically difficult position we would occupy in a war against the Entente. For the central military authorities to prepare for the possibility of a war which was, perhaps, unavoidable was certainly their duty so far as the people were concerned. That was what they were there for. And in the same way, they were under the obligation, in case a war turned out to be unavoidable, and in the course of the war itself, to make use of every possible chance.

We considered it to be our primary duty to end the war by military means as quickly as possible and as favorably to ourselves as possible, in order to make it possible for the political department, as soon as it could in any way be done, to again bring the life of the country into tune with the normal and peaceful methods of statesmanship. . . .

We knew what we would have to demand of the Army, of the officers of the highest and lower ranks, and, not least of all, of the man in the grey coat, and we know what they have all done. But in spite of the tremendous demands that were made upon the troops and upon leadership, in spite of the superiority of the enemy in point of numbers, we could have fought out the unequal conflict to a favorable termination if determined and unanimous cooperation on the part of those in the armies and those at home had been the case. It was in this circumstance that we discerned the means of gaining a victory for the German cause, on the attainment of which our minds were firmly set.

But what was it that happened? . . .

History will render its final judgment with regard to those matters concerning which I am to speak no further here. At that time, we still believed that the will to conquer over-rode every other consideration. When we took command, we submitted to the government a number of proposals, the purpose of which was to concentrate all our national forces for the purpose of bringing about an early termination of the war, and one that would be favorable to us; these proposals explained to the government the gigantic tasks which were ahead of us. However, we all know what the fate of our proposals came to be, and that this was, again, due in part to political influences. What I sought to obtain was strong and cheerful cooperation, and I was met with weakness and a refusal to act. . . .

From this moment on, we were never free from anxiety as to whether or not our people at home would stand fast until the war was won. Again and again we raised our voices in a warning directed to the government. It was at this time that plans were set on foot for the secret and deliberate disintegration of both fleet and army, as a step in furtherance of similar phenomena which had existed in times of peace. The results of these efforts during the last year of the war were not withheld from the knowledge of the Supreme High Command of the Army. The brave troops which kept themselves free from the contact of revolutionary deterioration were hard put to it, as the result of the mutinous attitude of their revolutionary comrades; they were called upon to bear the whole burden of the conflict. . . .

The purposes which the leaders contemplated became now impossible to carry out. Our repeated exhortations on behalf of strict discipline and the strict application of the laws met with no results. So our operations were bound to fail, and the collapse was bound to come; the revolution was but the keystone. . . .

An English general has said, with justice: "The German Army was stabbed in the back." No blame is to be attached to the sound core of the Army. Its performances call, like that of the officers' corps, for our equal admiration. It is perfectly plain on whom the blame lies.

HARLAN R. CRIPPEN
Military-Civilian Coalition

The following three selections refute much of what Hindenburg claimed in his testimony. The first selection indicates that the leaders of the German army were willing, for the present, to work with the new German government. At the same time, as selections two and three show, the army leaders wanted to accept absolutely no public responsibility for the signing of the armistice.

FRITZ EBERT is alone in the Chancellor's room. His friends have all gone. In sweat-soaked collar and unbuttoned waistcoat he sits back in the chair from which he has not moved for hours. The pace has been almost too much for him. In the morning he was still hopeful of saving the monarchy; by ten o'clock he was studying how to fall into the arms of the strikers; by noon all that remained was the plan for summoning a constituent assembly; by nightfall he is on the verge of losing the power to the Workers' and Soldiers' Councils. But he has prepared everything for the morrow and has no doubt that a cabinet of Social Democrats and Independents will

From Harlan R. Crippen, ed., *Germany: A Self-Portrayal; A Collection of German Writings from 1914 to 1934* (London: Oxford University Press, 1944), pp. 121-125.

come into being. And of such a cabinet an instrument can be forged which shall gradually override the Councils. What Noske has done for Kiel must now be done for Berlin, and for the Reich. It really boils down to a question of military power. The army which had stood behind the old government is breaking up. The soldiers will disperse to the four winds, no doubt, but the officers—what will they do? . . . The thought, which means treachery, is there again.

Ebert is free of exalted ideas and without the least inclination toward sentimentality. The 9th November—that day for which generations of Socialists have longed, for which so many have suffered—is safely behind him. It has not caused his blood to move a jot faster; it has merely made him dog tired.

And what is treachery?—an idle question without foundation in political realism, which ranters and idealists may care to answer. And what is socialism?—one ideal for the liberation of mankind; and of such there are many. Politics is not concerned with ideals. What concerns Ebert is not socialism, but the Social Democratic Party. And if the Workers' and Soldiers' Councils get the upper hand, this great instrument will surely come under the wheels and be ground to powder—unless—unless he can contrive at the right moment to get some military force to back his policy. Can he call the officers of the old imperial army to his aid?—that is the question.

Ebert gets up from his chair. He goes to the door, opens it and listens a moment in the passage, then shuts it again and locks it. He sinks back heavily into the armchair and looks long at the telephone before him. If he lifts the receiver, the exchange will answer; but if he first switches over himself, he is in touch by private line with G.H.Q. at Spa and can speak to the Quartermaster-General without anyone overhearing. . . .

If it were merely a question of the surrender of yet another socialist principle, of which so many have already had to be sacrificed to the exigencies of practical policy and that not on his initiative alone but with the full approval of every understanding colleague— But there you have it! those other steps had never been undertaken without the sanction of a majority.

And here he is alone.

Friedrich Ebert who has opposed bourgeois democracy to the desire of the working classes for single control, placing the decision as to the future destiny of the people in the hands of an elected Constituent Assembly to be called together by every capitalist device for influencing votes—Friedrich Ebert who, as a party official, has challenged every smallest independent action on the part of a colleague, and dragged up for censure before the Party Committee any functionary who, without previous permission, has bought for the use of his office so much as a curtain worth twelve marks fifty or, without observing all the details of prescribed routine, has acted on his own initiative in the most trifling affairs— Friedrich Ebert, whose blood had boiled only a few hours ago when Scheidemann, without previous party sanction, had proclaimed the Republic—Ebert now stands alone, face to face with the most crucial decision his party has ever had to make.

In small concerns Ebert has ever been painfully observant of every requirement of party discipline; in great matters he has more than once set himself above it, but never without a twinge of conscience. So now he sits in front of the telephone, a complex of tormenting inhibitions and thoughts—on the one hand, a successful military *coup,* the restoration of the Imperial Reich, court-martial for the rebellious workers; on the other, the power in the hands of the Workers' and Soldiers' Councils, the setting up of a German Republic of Councils, the overthrow of the capitalist system. —Ebert can decide neither for the one nor the other; he must find a middle path for his party.

His hand reaches for the receiver, then lets it lie.

Wait and see—those are the tactics which have brought him thus far—they will not fail him now.—He sinks back onto speculation and brooding. . . .

A telephone rings in the Chancellery.

The President of the Social Democratic Party has the receiver in his hand:

"Ebert speaking."

"Groener speaking."

Quartermaster-General Groener has consulted his staff and discussed the matter with Field-Marshal von Hindenburg. The army asks the support of the Social Democratic Party for the restoration of its lost authority. As a price, the Generals offer to the new Government the protection of their bayonets and guns.

Chancellor Ebert listens attentively to the First Quartermaster-General Groener's proposals. Then he asks:

"What is your attitude toward the Workers' and Soldiers' Councils?"

"Commanders have been instructed to deal with them in a friendly spirit."

"And what do you expect of us?"

"The General Field-Marshal expects the Government of the Reich to support the Officers' Corps in the maintenance of discipline and order in the army. He asks also that the provisioning of the army shall be ensured by every possible means and that any disturbance of railway communications shall be prevented."

"Anything else?"

"The Officers' Corps invites the Government of the Reich to fight Bolshevism, and for this purpose places itself at the Government's disposal."

Ebert hesitates before giving his answer. He looks up at the thickly padded door; he turns toward the window and listens for any sound from the street, where he fancies he already hears the enraged shouts of the workers.

Then in a confident voice he replies:

"Convey to the General Field-Marshal the thanks of the Government."

GORDON A. CRAIG
The High Command's Attitude

WHEN THE REPUBLIC was proclaimed on the afternoon of 9 November, the first quartermaster-general reacted with none of that instinctive horror that affected his professional colleagues. He had had enough dealings with the Social Democrats during the war to realize that they were not very ardent revolutionaries and that their attitude toward the radicals and separatists was not much different from his own. He suspected that, in their present insecure position, they would welcome an offer of military support. At the same time, it was obviously to the interest of the officer corps to have the vacuum left by the fall of the monarchy filled by some governmental authority with a claim to legitimacy. Unless the officers could argue that they were serving such authority, they might lose control of the troops to the soldiers councils, which were already established in the *Etappe* and were now springing up among the front-line regiments. Moreover, the Allied Powers had now transmitted the terms of armistice to the High Command; and Groener—concerned, as he wrote later, "with keeping our weapons clean and the General Staff

From *The Politics of the Prussian Army, 1640-1945* by Gordon A. Craig, Copyright 1955 by Gordon A. Craig. Reprinted by permission of Oxford University Press, Inc.

unburdened for the future"—needed a civilian government which would assume the responsibility for accepting them.[1]

These considerations led the first quartermaster-general on the night of 9 November to make his now famous telephone call to Friedrich Ebert, the leader of the Majority Socialists and the new Chancellor of the Reich. In the course of a brief conversation, he promised that the present High Command would continue its functions until the troops had been brought back to Germany in good order and perfect discipline. This was, at least implicitly, an admission that the army recognized the legitimacy of the new regime, but it was, nevertheless, a conditional recognition. Groener make it clear that the officer corps expected the government to aid it in maintaining discipline in the army, in securing the army's sources of supply, and in preventing the disruption of the railway system during the army's march home. And he stressed the fact that the officer corps looked to the government to combat bolshevism and was putting itself at the government's disposal primarily for that purpose.

Ebert accepted the offer and the conditions without hesitation, and thus the historic pact was concluded—a pact which, in the words of one authority, was "destined to save both parties from the extreme elements of revolution but, as a result of which, the Weimar Republic was doomed at birth."

[1]Groener's eagerness to avoid responsibility for terms which he knew would be harsh had already been shown on 6 November when he had agreed that the German armistice delegation should be headed by a civilian rather than a soldier. See General H. Mordacq, *L'Armistice du 11 Novembre 1918* (Paris, 1937), pp. 145-9. Harry Rudin's argument in *Armistice 1918* (New Haven, 1944), pp. 323-4 that the initiative for this change came from the civilian authorities, is true but loses its force in view of Groener's later statement that he "could only approve [an arrangement whereby], in these unhappy negotiation, from which no good was to be expected, the army and the army command remained as free from blame as possible." *Lebenserinnerungen,* p. 449.

JOHN W. WHEELER-BENNETT

Military Irresponsibility

NOR WAS THIS ALL. In Gröner's calculations on the night of November 9, there remained the all-important factor that for the last twenty-four hours a German delegation had been in negotiation with

From John W. Wheeler-Bennett, *The Nemesis of Power: The German Army in Politics, 1918-1945* (New York: St. Martin's Press, 1954), pp. 23-24.

Marshal Foch at Compiegne for the conclusion of an armistice. In the course of the pre-Armistice exchanges the Supreme Command, though they had initiated them by their demand of September 29 that a peace offer be dispatched forthwith, had sought to escape from their responsibility and had refused to have anything to do with the final appointment of the Armistice Commission. This pusillanimous attitude had been materially, if unintentionally, strengthened by the fact that President Wilson in his Note of November 5 had stated that Marshal Foch was prepared to receive properly accredited representatives *of the German Government* and to acquaint them with the Armistice conditions. Though consistent with the President's earlier statement (October 23) that the Allies could only treat with "the military masters and the monarchical autocrats of Germany" on the basis of unconditional surrender, this insistence now upon negotiation with representatives of the German Government played directly into the hands of the Supreme Command, who were thereby relieved of all responsibility, with the result that no representative of the General Staff was included in the Armistice Commission.[1] What is, perhaps, surprising is that their relief was shared by the Chancellor, Prince Max of Baden.

[1]The German Armistice Commission, of which Mathias Erzberger was president, did include one Army officer, Major-General von Winterfeldt, a former military attache at the German Embassy in Paris, who had been hurriedly brought out of retirement. He did not participate in the subsequent negotiations for the renewal of the Armistice. When the Commission had arrived at Spa on November 7, on its way to Compiegne, there had been a moment of hideous uncertainty on the part of the High Command lest Erzberger might at the last moment refuse to go and they might, after all, have to provide a substitute. General von Gündell had actually been warned for duty in this emergency, but Hindenburg, with tears in his eyes and grasping Erzberger by the hand, besought him to undertake this terrible task for the sacred cause of his country. His vanity flattered by this personal appeal from the Marshal, Erzberger consented to serve and departed to put his signature to a document which was to prove his own death-warrant. He was assassinated by Nationalist gunmen in 1921 for his part in the Armistice negotiations (Erzberger, *Erlebnisse im Weltkrieg* (Berlin, 1920), p. 326; Wheeler-Bennett *(op cit.),* pp. 188-9; Jacques Benoist-Mechin, *Histoire de l'armee allemande depuis l'armistice* (Paris, 1936-8), i. p. 41.) M. Benoist-Mechin (b. 1902), whose book is a classic on its subject and was *couronne* by the French Academy, was nominated, after the collapse of France in 1940, Delegate-General for Prisoners of War with residence in Berlin. Later, in Vichy, he served successively as Secretary of State to Admiral Darlan and to Laval, 1941-2. Arrested after the Liberation of France, he was tried as a collaborationist before the High Court of Justice and was condemned to death on June 6, 1947; this sentence was later commuted by President Vincent Auriol (July 30, 1947) to one of imprisonment for life with hard labour (see *Le Process Benoist-Mechin,* Paris, 1948).

For the Army, therefore, it was all important that the onus of responsibility for accepting the Armistice conditions in all their severity—and the text had been received at Spa on the afternoon of November 9—should remain with the Government and not with the General Staff, and for that purpose it was essential that a Government of some sort should exist in Berlin.

FRANZ NEUMANN
Perversion of Justice

The German army was not the only segment of German society that helped to undermine the Republic. Much of the blame must fall on the German judiciary. Franz Neumann, in *Behemoth,* outlines how the judiciary perverted justice for political ends and fostered a profound contempt for the value of justice in the German people.

ON THE VERY DAY that the revolution broke out in 1918, the counterrevolutionary party began to organize. It tried many forms and devices, but soon learned that it could come to power only with the help of the state machine and never against it. The Kapp Putsch of 1920 and the Hitler Putsch of 1923 had proved this.

In the center of the counter-revolution stood the judiciary. Unlike administrative acts, which rest on considerations of convenience and expediency, judicial decisions rest on law, that is on right and wrong, and they always enjoy the limelight of publicity. Law is perhaps the most pernicious of all weapons in political struggles, precisely because of the halo that surrounds the concepts of right and justice. . . . When it becomes "political," justice breeds hatred and despair among those it singles out for attack. Those whom it favors, on the other hand, develop a profound contempt for the very value of justice; they know that it can be purchased by the powerful. As a device for strengthening one political group at the expense of others, for eliminating enemies and assisting political allies, law then threatens the fundamental convictions upon which the tradition of our civilization rests.

From Franz Neumann, *Behemoth: The Structure and Practice of National Socialism* (London: Oxford University Press, 1942), pp. 20-23.

The technical possibilities of perverting justice for political ends are widespread in every legal system; in republican Germany, they were as numerous as the paragraphs of the penal code. Perhaps the chief reason lay in the very nature of criminal trials, for, unlike the American system, the proceedings were dominated not by counsel but by the presiding judge. The power of the judge, furthermore, was strengthened year after year. For political cases, the favorite statutory provisions were those dealing with criminal libel and espionage, the so-called Act for the Protection of the Republic, and, above all, the high treason sections (80 and 81) of the penal code. A comparative analysis of the three *causes celebres* will make it amply clear that the Weimar criminal courts were part and parcel of the anti-democratic camp.

After the downfall of the Bavarian Soviet Republic in 1919, the courts handed down the following sentences:

407 persons, fortress imprisonment
1737 persons, prison
65 persons, imprisoned at hard labor

Every adherent of the Soviet Republic who had the slightest connection with the unsuccessful coup was sentenced.

The contrast with the judicial treatment of the 1920 right-wing Kapp Putsch could not possibly have been more complete. Fifteen months after the putsch, the Reich ministry of justice announced officially on 21 May 1921 that a total of 705 charges of high treason had been examined. Of them,

412 in the opinion of the courts came under the amnesty law of 4 August 1920, despite the fact that the statute specifically excluded the putsch leaders from its provisions

108 had become obsolete because of death or other reasons

174 were not pressed

11 were unfinished

Not one person had been punished. Nor do the statistics give the full picture. Of the eleven cases pending on 21 May 1921, only one ended in a sentence; former Police President von Jagow of Berlin received five years' honorary confinement. When the Prussian state withdrew Jagow's pension, the federal supreme court ordered it restored to him. The guiding spirit of the putsch, Dr. Kapp, died before trial. Of the other leaders, some like General von Lüttwitz and Majors Papst and Bischoff escaped; General Ludendorff was not prosecuted because the court chose to accept his alibi that he was present only by accident; General von Lettow-Forbeck, who had occupied a whole town for Kapp, was declared to have been not a leader but merely a follower.

The third significant illustration is the judicial handling of Hitler's abortive Munich putsch of 1923. Hitler, Pöhner, Kriebel, and Weber received five years; Röhm, Frick, Brückner, Pernet and Wagner one year and three months. Ludendorff once again was present only by accident and was released. Although section 9 of the Law for the Protection of the Republic clearly and unmistakably ordered the deportation of every alien convicted of high treason, the Munich People's Court exempted Hitler on the specious argument that, despite his Austrian citizenship, he considered himself a German.

It would be futile to relate in detail the history of political justice under the Weimar Republic. A few more illustrations will suffice. The penal code created the crime of "treason to the country" to cover the betrayal of military and other secrets to foreign agents. The courts, however, promptly found a special political use for those provisions. After the Versailles Treaty forced Germany to disarm, the Reichswehr encouraged the formation of secret and illegal bodies of troops, the so-called "black Reichswehr." When liberals, pacifists, socialists, and communists denounced this violation of both international obligations and German law (for the treaty had become part of the German legal system), they were arrested and tried for treason to the country committed through the press. Thus did the courts protect the illegal and reactionary black Reichswehr. Assassinations perpetrated by the black Reichswehr against alleged traitors within their ranks (the notorious Fehme murders), on the other hand, were either not prosecuted at all or were dealt with lightly.

During the trials of National Socialists, the courts invariably became sounding boards for propaganda. When Hitler appeared as a witness at the trial of a group of National Socialist officers charged with high treason, he was allowed to deliver a two-hour harangue packed with insults against high government officials and threats against his enemies, without being arrested for contempt. The new techniques of justifying and publicizing National Socialism against the Weimar Republic were defended as steps designed to ward off the communist danger. National Socialism was the guardian of democracy, they shouted, and the courts were only too willing to forget the fundamental maxim of any democracy and of every state, that the coercive power must be a monopoly of the state through its army and police, that not even under the pretext of saving the state may a private group or individual take arms in its defense unless summoned to do so by the sovereign power or unless actual civil war has broken out.

In 1932 the police discovered a National Socialist plot in Hessen. A Dr. Best, now a high official in the regime, had worked out a careful plan for a *coup d'etat* and documentary proof was available (the Boxheimer documents). No action was taken. Dr. Best was believed when he stated that he intended to make use of his plan only in the event of a communist revolution.

It is impossible to escape the conclusion that political justice is the blackest page in the life of the German Republic. The judicial weapon was used by the reaction with steadily increasing intensity. Furthermore, this indictment extends to the entire record of the judiciary, and particularly to the change in legal thought and in the position of the judge that culminated in the new principle of judicial review of statutes (as a means of sabotaging social reforms). The power of the judges thereby grew at the expense of the parliament.

The Courts and the Nazis

Two accounts from the London *Times* illustrate the favoritism the judiciary showed to right wing groups. The first account is the trial of seventeen Communist sympathizers on charges of manslaughter in the death of a Nazi student, Horst Wessel. All the defendants received sentences ranging up to six years imprisonment. In the second trial three artillery subalterns attempted to win over army officers to the Nazi cause. For their treasonable undertaking the three officers received eighteen months detention.

AT THE MOABIT Criminal Court in Berlin today the trial opened of 17 persons, most of whom are associated with the Communist movement, on charges of manslaughter, complicity, or aiding and abetting, in the case of the National-Socialist student, Horst Wessel, who died in February from blood poisoning following a bullet

From *The Times* (London), 23 September 1930, p. 11 and 29 September 1930, p. 12.

wound he received a month earlier. Wessel took an ardent part in the "Nazi" movement. Höhler, who is accused of having fired the shot, was a leading member of a "storm detachment" of the proscribed Communist semi-military organization, the Red Fighting Front. Two other men, Rückert and Kandulski, are accused with Höhler of manslaughter. Of the 14 persons accused of complicity in varying degrees four are women. One of these, Frau Salm, was Wessel's landlady, and it was with her dispute with him about the flat that the trouble began. According to the indictment, Frau Salm, having failed to get Wessel and his sweetheart out of the flat, called upon Communists for help. Höhler, Rückert, and Kandulski went to Wessel's room, and as the door opened someone cried "Hands up!" A shot was fired almost simultaneously, and Wessel was hit in the mouth.

In evidence Frau Salm said that she saw some of the accused and asked for their support in her endeavor to get Wessel out of the flat. She told them Wessel was a Fascist, possessed two revolvers and a rubber truncheon, and constantly held meetings until the early hours of the morning in the flat. Of the actual shooting she professed to know nothing. Three Communists had gone to Wessel's door, she heard a shot and then the girl fetched her from the kitchen, and showed her Wessel lying bleeding on the floor of his room. She heard someone whisper, "Quick, all clear out."

Wessel asked for a doctor, Frau suggested one who was a Jew, whereupon a "Nazi" companion of Wessel's, who had in the meantime appeared, said that if a Jewish doctor came they would throw him downstairs. It was an hour or so before a doctor came who was regarded as satisfactory. Counsel for the defense said he proposed to submit expert evidence to show that Wessel would not have died of blood poisoning if he had been attended immediately by the Jewish physician who lived nearby.

In the afternoon several of the young Communists were heard. They explained that there had been no intention of shooting Wessel, it had merely been decided that Wessel should be given a "proletarian rub-down." According to Max Jambrowski, a Communist Party official, it was not decided to take arms; the proletarian storm detachments depended on their fists. He denied a statement made in the preliminary examination that he had nevertheless provided the money with which Höhler's revolver was bought. Asked what was understood by a "proletarian rub-down," he explained that "when we of the storm detachment decide to give

someone a 'proletarian rub-down,' we get together and deal with him so that he goes to hospital, but not with weapons, only with the fists."
The judge thought any further definition was unnecessary.

* * *

The Times correspondent at the end of his report on the Leipzig trial refers to the sentencing of 17 Communists charged with the murder of the Nazi student, Horst Wessel.
The 17 Communists charged with the manslaughter of a Nazi "storm detachment leader" having received on Friday terms of imprisonment varying between six years and four months, some Press criticism is directed at the lighter sentence passed on three Nazis who, during a non-political altercation with members of a football club, shot two men dead. They each received two years' imprisonment. At Coblenz on Friday a member of a Nazi "storm detachment" who had stabbed and killed a workman during altercation of obscure origin was sentenced to a year's imprisonment.

The Courts and the Communists

THE THREE ARTILLERY SUBALTERNS, Lieutenant (retired) Wendt and Second Lieutenants Ludin and Scheringer, who have been on trial before the Supreme Court at Leipzig, were yesterday sentenced to 18 months' fortress detention each for "jointly preparing a highly treasonable undertaking." The two active officers are to be dismissed the service.
Women waved and kissed their hands to the prisoners when the verdict was read. The President of the Court, after threatening unruly members of the public with arrest, then read the judgment.
He said that Lieutenants Scheringer and Ludin thought that the Army, like the people, was moving too far towards the Left and they went to Munich to commune with Nazi leaders about these matters. On their return they told Lieutenant Wendt of their journey and they decided "to win over officers in centrally situated areas who would

From *The Times* (London), 6 October 1930, p. 13.

maintain communication between themselves and comrades of similar views." The Court did not think these discussions were of a harmless nature.

At this point, the news of the verdict having become known, there was an uproar in the Reichsgerichtsplatz, where a large crowd had gathered, and cries of "Revenge!" and "Germany, Awake" drowned all other sounds. Students from the adjacent University arrived, and added to the tumult, and the square had to be cleared by mounted and foot police, who made a few arrests.

The President of the Court, continuing when quiet was restored, summarized the intentions of the accused, as revealed by the evidence, as follows: Reichswehr opposition to the patriotic associations in an eventual new *Putsch* must be avoided. The lieutenants were to canvass brother officers in this sense, and their journeys to distant garrisons were undoubtedly for this purpose. The treasonable activity of the accused was directed against a Government which they dislike. They wished to dissuade the Reichswehr from opposing the Nazi attempt to overthrow this Government. It was a foolish and Utopian plan, but nevertheless it was a plan. There were no extenuating circumstances, though the Court had taken account of the nobility of their motives. The accused heard the verdict and speech calmly; and received gifts of flowers from friends in Court before being led away.

In Munich, the home of the Nazis, the verdict has been received with violent protests, and Nazi placards on the advertisement kiosks are already attacking the "Berlin bureau generals" and this "political judgment."

HANNAH VOGT
Failure of the Parties

Hannah Vogt, in *Burden of Guilt*, summarizes the structure, attitudes, and position of the major political parties of the Weimar Republic. She concludes that the failure of these parties to find a middle way between impractical dogmas and narrowly egotistical interests aided the opponents of the democratic process in Germany. This is true even of those parties which were theoretically committed to the democracy.The political parties, therefore, must also share in the responsibility for the advent of Hitler.

THE DEMOCRATIC FORCES could not rely on those institutions whose manifest duty was to stay out of party politics and remain absolutely loyal to the Republic. Yet, the democratic position was not totally unfavorable at the start. Forces friendly to democracy formed a compact and promising majority. In the first parliament of 1920, the democratic parties collectively had captured 82 per cent of the popular vote; in the last free *Reichstag* election of 1932, a mere 39 per cent remained. These two figures reveal the tragic fate of a democracy which could find no middle way between impractical dogmas and overly narrow egotistical interests.

Of all democratic parties in the Weimar Republic, the Social Democratic Party (SPD) attracted the largest number of members. Its tenets were based on long historical tradition, and it was a close-knit organization, consisting of party workers and leaders, many of whom had proven their worth in the trade-union movement. Its program, originating from Marx and Engels, advocated a classless society and equal opportunities for all. In the course of several decades the party's program for achieving these goals had changed several times. Since a large portion of votes had gone to the SPD, a revolution was unnecessary, as the peaceful conquest and penetration of the state appeared to be within reach. Along these lines, the SPD pursued a very moderate and sober policy, and gave some internal stability to the democratic Republic after 1918.

When the Communists, under Moscow's control, began to organize themselves and gain influence, the SPD's struggle for the labor vote faced new difficulties. The Communists claimed that they alone interpreted Marxist theory correctly, whereas the SPD "betrayed" the dogma of the revolution as well as the workers. Under such competitive pressures from the left, the SPD failed to adjust its traditional views of the class struggle to the new social realities. At times this created the situation where SPD deputies in the *Reichstag,* in deference to their Marxist voters, were obliged to vote against propsals made by ministers of their own party.

The gulf between ideal and reality was felt especially by younger people. Many of them were attracted by Communist logic and the opportunities for a rapid rise to political leadership. Demagogues of the right-wing parties made their own use of this by equating Social Democrats with Communists and frightening the citizenry with the "Red menace." Thus it was possible that as the years went by, the SPD which had entered the Weimar National Assembly with 38 per cent of the vote was reduced to 20 per cent in the election of November 6, 1932, in spite of its excellent organization and a faithful core of voters.

The second largest party—the Center Party—was also the most stable. As a Catholic party, it drew votes from all strata of society. This forced it to compromise between various interests *within* the party, and it made it typically a moderate, middle-of-the-road party. It played an important part in the Weimar Republic, since its position in the center of the political spectrum meant that no government could be formed at any time against its interests, or without its participation. A frequent ally of the Center Party was the Bavarian People's Party, which had been founded by Bavarian deputies of the Center Party and which favored states' rights, at times to the detriment of common party interests. In all parliaments of the Weimar Republic, the Center Party and the Bavarian People's Party together controlled about 15 to 20 per cent of the votes.

In sharp contrast was the liberal German Democratic Party, which counted among its ranks some of the most outstanding personalities—Friedrich Naumann, Theodore Heuss, Max Weber, and Walther Rathenau. It had controlled 19 per cent of the votes in the National Assembly, but soon lost half of its votes and declined to an insignificant minority. In the last free *Reichstag* elections, the German Democratic Party, under its new name of States Party *(Staatspartei),* did not even poll 1 per cent of the popular vote. German voters had little love for the liberal program offered by the party, and so it turned into a so-called "party of notables" attracting some top brains, but few members.

A somewhat more right-wing liberalism was for a while, with visible success, represented by the German People's Party which had gathered up the former National Liberals and had attracted Gustav Stresemann as its most outstanding political leader. In the National Assembly, it had won only 4 per cent of the vote and, as early as the Reichstag elections of 1920, voted in large numbers for the Nationalists. For a time the party retained 8 per cent to 10 per cent of the vote, until 1932, when it shared the fate of the German Democratic Party and was crushed between extremists.

All the hopes of the young democracy rested on these four parties—the Social Democratic Party, the German Democratic Party, the Center Party, and the German People's Party. They entered into various changing coalitions with each other, and formed altogether 17 governments, including the Brüning government of 1932. Seven times, the SPD was represented in these governments, but the government was composed more frequently of parliamentary minorities obliged to rely upon the SPD—not itself a member of the government—for support if it wanted to retain office. Such an ill-defined situation, which knew no clear lines of responsibility nor a loyal opposition (both left and right opposition parties were destructive), did little to win the voting masses for democracy.

Even more confusing was the distressingly large number of small, even minute, splinter groups clinging to the major parties. They did not advocate programs hostile to the Republic, or to democracy, but used the opportunities offered by universal suffrage for the sole purpose of exploiting the *Reichstag* as a sounding board for their special interests. Among these notorious 27 or 28 parties in the Weimar Republic there were some whose aims had nothing to do with genuine politics. This is demonstrated by titles such as "Revalorization Party," or a "Tenants' League," a "House-and Land-Owners Party," or a "Peasants" and "Vintners' League," etc. The largest of these groups, the "Economy Party," represented the interests of the middle classes. The large parties often needed these groups to form their coalitions, with the result that the influence of these groups in politics was out of all proportion to their true importance.

A glance at a ballot of this period explains why the voters were appalled by this turmoil, why they felt that parties did not represent the will of the people, but merely served as a pretext for selfish interests. Hitler's task was rendered easier by the already deep dissatisfaction with the existing party system.

ARNOLD J. HEIDENHEIMER
Republican Government without Republicans

Arnold Heidenheimer's *Governments of Germany* supports Vogt's theories on the political parties. Heidenheimer, however, devotes more time to the government structure. He comments on the failure of the Reichstag and president to delineate responsibility. The cabinet, furthermore, had very little power against a demanding legislature on the one hand, and an arbitrary executive on the other. Heidenheimer, like Vogt, concludes that in the end it was the failure of the democratic forces to redirect their energies from the effective criticism of an authoritarian state to the effective strengthening of a democratic state.

AFTER THE DOWNFALL of the Emperor's regime, Germans were suddenly presented with the opportunity to follow the dominant political tradition of the West by establishing democratic political institutions. Surprisingly, the opportunity caught most German political parties unprepared. Even the progressive groups had prepared only piecemeal reform plans looking at most toward a constitutional monarchy. There were virtually no republicans. Earlier liberal democratic sentiment had atrophied or been stunted. Of all the German parties only one carried the word "democratic" in its name, and this by its program was pledged to achieve a socialist revolution. To most Germans domestic democrats seemed like political animals out of the dim pre-Bismarckian past. They thought of great-grandfathers who in the early nineteenth century had cursed into their beer at the arrogance of the local prince, or had climbed grandiloquently onto makeshift barricades in the picture-book revolutions of 1848.

In the interval, the vast bulk of educated German opinion had drawn broad philosophical conclusions from limited historical experience, so that they saw in the decay of liberal movements proof that democratic forms were not suited to German politics. The experiences of the Western countries were dismissed as inapplicable. The German upper-middle class tended to share the snobbish ethos of the old ruling classes, who looked askance at Britain as a country of traders where even the nobility had accepted mercantile values. Parliamentary institutions were conceived as suitable for the compromise of sordid economic interests, but not adequate for a nation of poets and philosophers. As Thomas Mann wrote in 1918: "Away with the foreign and repulsive slogan 'democratic.' The mechanical democratic political institutions of the West will never take root here." . . .

Having split with their own left wing, the majority of the Socialists cooperated in drafting the constitution with the two other parties which by 1919 had accepted the republic, namely, the progressive German Democratic party (DDP) and the Catholic Center party *(Zentrum)*. That the constitution was to bear a primarily liberal democratic, rather than Socialist, character was borne out by the fact that the drafting work was entrusted to a Democratic party constitutional law professor. There was wide agreement that the constitution should establish a parliamentary system, but little in the way of German traditions to build on. Looking abroad, the drafters found appeal in the relative stability of British governments, but mistakenly attributed this to a constitutional balance of power between the King and Parliament. Thus they concentrated on creating a constitutional figure, the president, who would take the place of the British monarch as the authoritative balancing force which could help shape order out of the diversity of opinions represented in the powerful and popularly elected legislature. . . .

Structurally, the experiment with the creation of a dual authority, Reichstag and president, neither of which carried executive responsibility, was a dubious one. The two Weimar presidents were distrusted by large segments of the population; Friedrich Ebert (1919-1925), because he was a Socialist ex-saddler, Otto von Hindenburg (1925-1934), because he was a conservative ex-general. Most precarious of all was the constitutional position of that organ which was most important in shaping the political prestige of the regime. For the cabinet was given little power to maintain itself against a demanding legislature, and successive ministries found themselves at the mercy of either the president's pleasure, or shifting legislative majorities, or both. The weakness of the cabinet, moreover, was directly related to the functioning of the party system, which the Constitution's drafters did not adequately take into account. In order to stay in power, cabinets had to retain the confidence of a legislative majority, which meant the confidence of parties. Parties were thus the supremely important institutions, but the Constitution neither recognized nor regulated their position. The stability of the larger democratic parties was threatened by the ease with which splinter groups could sap their strength because of the prevailing system of proportional representation, which allowed even minute parties to gain parliamentary representation. Finally, the ease with which anti-constitutional parties could contribute to the overthrow of successive governments made the position of the parties supporting the regime increasingly difficult. . . .

The Weimar Constitution might nevertheless have served as the basis for a stable democratic state if subsequent political conditions had been more favorable. As it was, the antidemocratic groups were given an initial advantage by the fact that the democratic parties, who acted as midwives to the Constitution, also had to take responsibility for accepting what practically all Germans regarded as a humiliating and ruthless peace treaty. "Versailles" became a club for the extreme nationalist groups which soon organized amidst the chaos caused by civil strife and economic hardship, followed by ruinous inflation. By arguing that "traitors" on the home-front had caused defeat by stabbing the army in the back, the extremists won the cooperation of many reactionary officers, who had lost economic position and social status as a result of the virtual disbanding of the German army. (The peace treaty provided for a Reichswehr of only 100,000.) The nationalist fanatics showed their determination by assassinating some of the most prominent of the new republic's statesmen, including the ministers Erzberger and Rathenau, who belonged respectively to the Center and Democratic parties. Further difficulties for the regime were caused by the French occupation of the Rhineland and the need to pay large reparations to the victor nations, in addition to having to renounce claim to all German colonies.

By the mid-twenties, however, the regime was beginning to gain stability amid world-wide prosperity. The working class reaffirmed its support of the moderate constitutional policies of the Social Democrats, who remained the most solid backbone of the regime. The SPD (Sozialdemokratische Partei Deutschlands) discarded much of its semirevolutionary ideology and, together with the dominant trade union movement to which it was affiliated, supplied the bulk of the mass electorate, local officials, and grass roots support which sustained the regime among the people. From its ranks also came most of the volunteers who joined the prorepublican organizations which kept the Nazi and Communist street gangs in check. The other of the two original "Weimar" or prorepublican parties proved less stable. Most of the German Democratic party's middle-class voters deserted it in the course of the twenties, mainly in favor of two more conservative parties, the moderate right-wing German Peoples' party (DVP) and the nationalist-Protestant German National Peoples' party (DNVP), whose attitude toward the republic was much more critical. Gradually these two parties shared in assuming governmental responsibility, and the DVP even produced the single outstanding parliamentary figure of the Weimar Republic, Gustav Stresemann, who as Foreign Minister went furthest in seeking to strengthen German ties to the Western world, particularly to France. Cabinets including representatives of these parties alternated throughout the twenties. Even the victory in the 1925 elections for the presidency of the right-wing parties' candidate, Hindenburg, caused no grave concern, for the venerable ex-general pledged himself to support the republican Constitution. . . .

But while considerable portions of the educated elite served as the republic's grave-diggers, the most direct threats were to come from political movements which attracted large segments of the masses. Leading the groups which sought to destroy democracy through the use of democratic elections were the National Socialists and the Communists. Both recruited strong cores of members dedicated to the establishment, respectively, of Fascist or proletarian dictatorships. But, though well organized and able to agitate with relative impunity, these movements proved no serious threat during the period of prosperity. In 1928 the total anticonstitutional vote of these and similar movements was less than 15 per cent. (The Nazis polled only 2.6 per cent.) But the repercussions of the world depression aggravated the underlying economic and social tensions. The failure of the market mechanism seemed to lend support to those prophets of doom who had long predicted that both liberal democracy and capitalism were on their last legs. Large social groups became disaffected because of very severe grievances. Small businessmen felt themselves driven to ruin by the bankers and the cartels. Farmers rallied to use force to prevent foreclosures. Skilled artisans rebelled against the pressure to join the industrial proletariat or even the long line of the unemployed. Workers of all kinds lent a ready ear to radical exhortation, as the cutbacks in production cost them their jobs and the government's attempt to maintain balanced budgets cut into their meagre unemployment benefits. University-trained intellectuals and technicians, unable to find responsible jobs, joined the antidemocratic forces in droves, and the universities became hotbeds of radicalism, mainly of the rightist kind. Finally, the disgruntled among the insecure lower-middle classes rallied in large numbers to the siren songs of the splinter groups and the totalitarian movements.

Under the resulting pressures, the party alliances which had supported the regime began to crumble. Interest groups within the larger parties made irreconcilable demands and frequently split off into special interest parties. On election day the voter was wooed by as many as twenty parties. The air was full of party strife as policies based on economic interest calculations were superimposed on older programs based on ideological traditions. If there was little agreement on substantive questions there was even less on procedural ones. Extremist groups espoused a variety of radical solutions. Among the larger parties, the DNVP and the DVP began to edge away from their earlier, partial commitment to the Constitution and called for the creation of a presidential regime and other strong-man solutions. The workers shifted their strength from the Socialists to the Communists. But the biggest gains were made by the Nazis.

The real political crisis of the republic began with the 1930 elections, brought about by the inability of the democratic parties to agree on basic economic policies. They showed a sharp increase of public support for both the right-wing and Nazi parties (the latter jumped from 12 to 107 seats) which began to coalesce into a powerful anticonstitutional force. Viewed with suspicion by the moderate left and denied the cooperation of the right, the Center party Chancellor, Heinrich Bruening, sustained his government even without the support of a parliamentary majority, as a result of President Hindenburg's delegation of powers to rule by emergency decree. From that point on, government on the basis of democratic legitimation ceased, and administration based on a negative impasse began. . . . In July, 1932, after they had succeeded in forcing new Reichstag elections which resulted in their capture of 230 Reichstag seats, they became by far the largest party. At this point the pro-democratic parties ceased to be influential forces altogether. . . .

With the wisdom of hindsight, we can easily deduce that the German democratic system of the interwar period was not adequately prepared to sustain itself against the threat of totalitarian movements seeking to capture it from within. But can we pinpoint the faults? Was the constitutional system badly designed, or was distortion caused by the political forces which operated it? Were the electoral machinery and party leaders at fault, or were the Germans so hopelessly divided that neither leadership nor constitutional devices could save them? Was the republic doomed because of the German's want of experience with self-government and lack of commitment to democratic values, or because powerful minority groups unscrupulously encouraged a demagogic leader's mad ambitions? Experts are still very much divided on these questions, but a number of statements can be made about the lessons of Weimar, especially as perceived by those Germans who sought to reinstate democracy after the Nazi regime had collapsed:

(1) The Germans' first national experiment with self-government occurred both under extraordinarily unfavorable circumstances and at a time when too many Germans were still too divided on too many basic political ends, as well as on how to achieve them. A basic prerequisite of parliamentary democracy is a wide consensus on national goals, or at least on acceptable alternatives. This did not exist in Germany for most of the period of the republic.

(2) German political and interest group organizations, and especially the leaders who guided them, were not well adapted to functioning within a democratic system. Too much influenced by outdated ideological systems and/or narrow concern for special interests, they were unable to grow beyond their earlier subordinate positions and to produce leaders who could define, shape, and confront the larger issues. Even parties which were intellectually committed to democracy proved unable to redirect their energies from the effective criticism of an authoritarian state to the effective strengthening of a democratic state.

LOUIS L. SNYDER
Runaway Inflation

Louis Snyder outlines the background to the 1923 inflation in Germany.
No other country has ever experienced an inflation comparable to that
of Germany in 1923. This inflation caused the proletarianization of the
middle classes and initiated their support of either extreme right wing
or left wing groups.

FRENCH OCCUPATION of the Ruhr triggered an economic breakdown which led eventually to the collapse of the German mark.
Before the war the mark was valued at 4.2 per dollar. During the war
the mark began to drop slowly. The longer the British blockade
continued, the greater became the volume of currency. This was not
considered dangerous, for a certain amount of inflation took place
during any protracted conflict. In 1919 the mark stood at 8.9 per
dollar. Germany ended the war with a national debt of 144 billion
marks, of which 89 billion were in long-term bonds and 55 billion in
paper.

The inflationary situation was worsened by the great cost of
demobilization and the confused events of the revolution. The
presses began to print paper money faster and faster. At first,
industrialists and merchants, even the general public, were not
aware of the creeping inflation. The flood of new money swept
shelves free of merchandise. The stock market became increasingly
active.

By the middle of 1923 the value of the mark began to assume
astronomical proportions. In November 1923 the mark sank to the
value of 42 hundred million to the dollar. Prices began to rise
tenfold, a hundred times, in a single day. A hundred-mark bill one
day became a million-mark paper note the next day. The American
dollar became the measure of value, and prices were adjusted to it
rather than to the mark. Soon the printing presses could not keep up
with the changing need for paper money. City governments began to
issue their own emergency money printed on silk, linen, and even
leather *(Notgeld)*. Private concerns were given permission to over-
print paper money. More than three hundred paper mills and two

thousand printing shops worked around the clock to supply bank notes.

Germany was in a veritable fever dance. There were extraordinary scenes. A woman who came to her butcher shop with a basketful of marks left them on the pavement as she followed the queue inside to get her meat. On her return she found her marks dumped into the gutter and the basket stolen. On streetcar rides the conductor did not accept fares until the end of the ride because the value of the mark would change in a matter of minutes. One could buy a night club or obtain the Emperor's box at the opera with a few dollar bills. Housewives had to shop several times a day, because a pound of butter might rise five times in cost within 24 hours. A week's subscription to a newspaper might cost a billion marks. Workers had to exchange six-weeks' pay (carted in wheelbarrows) for a pair of shoes. At one time it cost a billion marks to send a letter abroad.

There was a wild scramble for real goods of any kind. Barter replaced the money economy in many parts of the country. Huge fortunes were acquired within a few months by those who had access to foreign currencies. The effect was catastrophic for those with fixed incomes—with bank accounts, insurance policies, and pensions. The people who were wiped out lost all sense of security. The productive middle class, traditionally the backbone of the country, was deprived of its property. Widows, civil servants, teachers, army officers, and pensioners lost their lifetime savings. Such unfortunates held tenaciously to their white-collar status to avoid being thrust down into the ranks of the despised proletariat. It was the scar that never healed. These were the people who later turned to Adolf Hitler as the messiah to lead them out of financial chaos.

It is incorrect and unjust to charge the German government with complicity in bringing about the inflation deliberately in order to pay reparations. The process of inflation was already under way when the French occupied the Ruhr. The French action merely accelerated the avalanche. The German government did contribute unwittingly by its reluctance to raise taxes at a time when reconstruction and welfare schemes were financed through deficit spending. Municipal improvements were financed through the issue of paper money rather than an increase in taxes. This helped unbalance the economy. The abolition of the gold standard, on August 4, 1914, also contributed to the inflationary process.

The entire problem was closely connected with the reparations demanded by the Allies from Germany for damage caused during the war. The Allies wanted no paper money: they were interested only in German productive capacity. Both Allied and German leaders learned the hard way, after the damage had been done, that the transfer of huge amounts of money in a highly unstable economy leads to critical economic dislocation.

STEFAN ZWEIG
An Episode of the Inflation

Stefan Zweig's *The Invisible Collection* is a short story about the effects of the 1923 inflation on a lower middle class family. His story is typical of the fate suffered by many of the declassed bourgeoisie.

AT THE FIRST JUNCTION beyond Dresden, an elderly gentleman entered our compartment, smiled genially to the company, and gave me a special nod, as if to an old acquaintance. Seeing that I was at a loss, he mentioned his name. Of course I knew him! He was one of the most famous connoisseurs and art-dealers in Berlin. Before the war, I had often purchased autographs and rare books at his place. He took the vacant seat opposite me, and for a while we talked of matters not worth relating. Then, changing the conversation, he explained the object of the journey from which he was returning. It had, he said, been one of the strangest of his experiences in the thirty-seven years he had devoted to the occupation of art-pedlar. Enough introduction. I will let him tell the story in his own words, without using quote-marks—to avoid the complication of wheels within wheels.

You know (he said) what has been going on in my trade since the value of money began to diffuse into the void like gas. War-profiteers have developed a taste for old masters (Madonnas and so on), for incunabula, for ancient tapestries. It is difficult to satisfy their craving; and a man like myself, who prefers to keep the best

From Stefan Zweig, *The Invisible Collection*, in *Heart of Europe: An Anthology of Creative Writing in Europe, 1920-1940*, ed. by Klaus Mann and Hermann Kesten (New York: L. B. Fisher, 1943), pp. 592-602.

for his own use and enjoyment, is hard put to it not to have his house stripped bare. If I let them, they would buy the cuff-links from my shirts and the lamp from my writing-table. Harder and harder to find wares to sell. I'm afraid the term "wares" may grate upon you in this connexion, but you must excuse me. I have picked it up from customers of the new sort. Evil communications . . . . Through use and wont I have come to look upon an invaluable book from one of the early Venetian presses much as the philistine looks upon an overcoat that cost so or so many hundred dollars, and upon a sketch by Guercino as animated by nothing more worthy of reverence than the transmigrated soul of a banknote for a few thousand francs.

Impossible to resist the greed of these fellows with money to burn. As I looked round my place the other night, it seemed to me that there was so little left of any real value that I might as well put up the shutters. Here was a fine business which had come down to me from my father and grandfather; but the shop was stocked with rubbish which, before 1914, a street-trader would have been ashamed to hawk upon a handcart.

In this dilemma, it occurred to me to flutter the pages of our old ledgers. Perhaps I should be put on the track of former customers who might be willing to resell what they had bought in prosperous days. True, such a list of sometime purchases has considerable resemblance to a battlefield laden with the corpses of the slain; and in fact I soon realized that most of those who had purchased from the firm when the sun was shining were dead or would be in such low water that it was probable they must have sold anything of value among their possessions. However, I came across a bundle of letters from a man who was presumably the oldest yet alive—if he was alive. But he was so old that I had forgotten him, since he had bought nothing after the great explosion in the summer of 1914. Yes, very, very old. The earliest letters were dated more than half a century back, when my grandfather was head of the business. Yet I could not recall having had any personal relationships with him during the thirty-seven years in which I had been an active worker in the establishment.

All indications showed that he must have been one of those antediluvian eccentrics, a few of whom survive in German provincial towns. His writing was copperplate, and every item in his orders was underlined in red ink. Each price was given in words as well as figures, so that there could be no mistake. These peculiarities, and his use of torn-out fly-leaves as writing paper, enclosed in a scratch assortment of envelopes, hinted at the penuriousness of a confirmed backwoodsman. His signature was always followed by his style and title in full: "Forest Ranger and Economic Councillor, Retired; Lieutenant, Retired; Holder of the Iron Cross First Class." Since he was obviously a veteran of the war of 1870-1871, he must be by now close on eighty.

For all his cheese-paring and for all his eccentricities, he had manifested exceptional shrewdness, knowledge, and taste as collector of prints and engravings. A careful study of his orders, which had at first totalled very small sums indeed, disclosed that in the days when a taler could still pay for a pile of lovely German woodcuts, this country bumpkin had got together a collection of etchings and the like outrivalling the widely trumpeted acquisitions of war profiteers. Merely those which, in the course of decades, he had bought from us for trifling sums would be worth a large amount of money today; and I had no reason to suppose that he had failed to pick up similar bargains elsewhere. Was his collection dispersed? I was too familiar with what had been going on in the art trade since the date of his last purchase not to feel confident that such a collection could scarcely have changed hands entire without my getting wind of the event. If he was dead, his treasures had probably remained intact in the hands of his heirs.

The affair seemed so interesting that I set forth next day (yesterday evening) on a journey to one of the most out-of-the-way towns in Saxony. When I left the tiny railway station and strolled along the main street, it seemed to me impossible that anyone inhabiting one of these gimcrack houses, furnished in a way with which you are doubtless familiar, could possibly own a full set of magnificent Rembrandt etchings together with an unprecedented number of Dürer woodcuts and a complete collection of Mantegnas. However, I went to the post-office to inquire, and was astonished to learn that a sometime Forest Ranger and Economic Councillor of the name I mentioned was still living. They told me how to find his house, and I will admit that my heart beat faster than usual as I made my way thither. It was well before noon.

The connoisseur of whom I was in search lived on the second floor of one of those jerry-built houses which were run up in such numbers by speculators during the sixties of the last century. The first floor was occupied by a master tailor. On the second landing to the left was the nameplate of the manager of the local post-office, while the porcelain shield on the right-hand door bore the name of my quarry. I had run him to earth! My ring was promptly answered by a very old, white-haired woman wearing a black lace cap. I handed her my card and asked whether the master was at home. With an air of suspicion she glanced at me, at the card, and then back at my face once more. In this Godforsaken little town a visit from an inhabitant of the metropolis was a disturbing event. However, in as friendly a tone as she could muster, she asked me to be good enough to wait a minute or two in the hall, and vanished through a doorway. I heard whispering, and then a loud, hearty, masculine voice: "Herr Rackner from Berlin, you say, the famous dealer in antiquities? Of course I shall be delighted to see him." Thereupon the old woman reappeared and invited me to enter.

I took off my overcoat, and followed her. In the middle of the cheaply furnished room was a man standing up to receive me. Old but hale, he had a bushy moustache and was wearing a semi-military, frogged smoking-jacket. In the most cordial way, he held out both hands towards me. But though this gesture was spontaneous and nowise forced, it was in strange contrast with the stiffness of his attitude. He did not advance to meet me, so that I was compelled (I must confess I was a trifle piqued) to walk right up to him before I could shake. Then I noticed that his hand, too, did not seek mine, but was waiting for mine to clasp it. At length I guessed what was amiss. He was blind.

Ever since I was a child I have been uncomfortable in the presence of the blind. It embarrasses me, produces in me a sense of bewilderment and shame to encounter anyone, who is thoroughly alive, and yet has not the full use of his senses. I feel as if I were taking an unfair advantage, and I was keenly conscious of this sensation as I glanced into the fixed and sightless orbs beneath the bristling white eyebrows. The blind man, however, did not leave me time to dwell upon this discomfort. He exclaimed, laughing with boisterous delight:

"A red-letter day, indeed! Seems almost a miracle that one of the big men of Berlin should drop in as you have done. There's need for us provincials to be careful, you know, when a noted dealer such as yourself is on the war-path. We've a saying in this part of the world: 'Shut your doors and button up your pockets if there are gipsies about!' I can guess why you've taken the trouble to call. Business doesn't thrive, I've gathered. No buyers or very few, so people are looking up their old customers. I'm afraid you'll draw a blank. We pensioners are glad enough to find there's still some dry bread for dinner. I've been a collector in my time, but now I'm out of the game. My buying days are over."

I hastened to tell him he was under a misapprehension, that I had not called with any thought of effecting sales. Happening to be in the neighbourhood I felt loath to miss the chance of paying my respects to a long-standing customer who was at the same time one of the most famous among German collectors. Hardly had the phrase passed my lips when a remarkable change took place in the old man's expression. He stood stiffly in the middle of the room, but his face lighted up and his whole aspect was suffused with pride. He turned in the direction where he fancied his wife to be, and nodded as if to say, "D'you hear that?" Then, turning back to me, he resumed—having dropped the brusque, drill-sergeant tone he had previously used, and speaking in a gentle, nay, almost tender voice:

"How charming of you. . . . I should be sorry, however, if your visit were to result in nothing more than your making the personal acquaintanceship of an old buffer like myself. At any rate I've something worth while for you to see—more worth while than you could find in Berlin, in the Albertina at Vienna, or even in the Louvre (God's curse on Paris!). A man who has been a diligent collector for fifty years, with taste to guide him, gets hold of treasures that are not to be picked up at every street-corner. Lisbeth, give me the key of the cupboard, please."

Now a strange thing happened. His wife, who had been listening with a pleasant smile, was startled. She raised her hands towards me, clasped them imploringly, and shook her head. What these gestures signified was a puzzle to me. Next she went up to her husband and touched his shoulder, saying:

"Franz, dear, you have forgotten to ask our visitor whether he may not have another appointment; and, anyhow, it is almost dinner-time. —I am sorry," she went on, looking to me, "that we have not enough in the house for an unexpected guest. No doubt you will dine at the inn. If you will take a cup of coffee with us afterwards, my daughter Anna Maria will be here, and she is much better acquainted than I am with the contents of the portfolios."

"Once more she glanced piteously at me. It was plain that she wanted me to refuse the proposal to examine the collection there and then. Taking my cue, I said that in fact I had a dinner engagement at the Golden Stag, but should be only too delighted to return at three, when there would be plenty of time to examine anything Herr Kronfeld wanted to show me. I was not leaving before six o'clock.

The veteran was as pettish as a child deprived of a favourite toy. "Of course," he growled, "I know you mandarins from Berlin have extensive claims on your time. Still, I really think you will do well to spare me a few hours. It is not merely two or three prints I want to show you, but the contents of twenty-seven portfolios, one for each master, and all of them full to bursting. However, if you come at three sharp, I dare say we can get through by six."

The wife saw me out. In the entrance hall, before she opened the front door, she whispered:

"Do you mind if Anna Maria comes to see you at the hotel before you return? It will be better for various reasons which I cannot explain just now."

"Of course, of course, a great pleasure. Really, I am dining alone, and your daughter can come along directly you have finished your own meal."

An hour later, when I had removed from the dining-room to the parlour of the Golden Stag, Anna Maria Kronfeld arrived. An old maid, wizened and diffident, plainly dressed, she contemplated me with embarrassment. I did my best to put her at her ease, and expressed my readiness to go back with her at once, if her father was impatient, though it was short of the appointed hour. At this she reddened, grew even more confused, and then stammered a request for a little talk before we set out.

"Please sit down," I answered. "I am entirely at your service."

She found it difficult to begin. Her hands and her lips trembled. At length:

"My mother sent me. We have to ask a favour of you. Directly you get back, Father will want to show you his collection; and the collection . . . the collection. Well, there's very little of it left."

She panted, almost sobbed, and went on breathlessly:

"I must be frank. . . . You know what troublous times we are passing through, and I am sure you will understand. Soon after the war broke out, my father became completely blind. His sight had already been failing. Agitation, perhaps, contributed. Though he was over seventy, he wanted to go to the front, remembering the fight in which he had taken part so long ago. Naturally there was no use for his services. Then, when the advance of our armies was checked, he took the matter very much to heart, and the doctor thought that may have precipitated the oncoming of blindness. In other respects, as you will have noticed, he is vigorous. Down to 1914 he could take long walks, and go out shooting. Since the failure of his eyes, his only pleasure is in his collection. He looks at it every day. 'Looks at it,' I say, though he sees nothing. Each afternoon he has the portfolios on the table, and fingers the prints one by one, in the order which many years have rendered so familiar. Nothing else interests him. He makes me read reports of auctions; and the higher the prices, the more enthusiastic does he become.

"There's the dreadful feature of the situation. Father knows nothing about the inflation; that we are ruined; that his monthly pension would not provide us with a day's food. Then we have others to support. My sister's husband was killed at Verdun, and there are four children. These money troubles have been kept from him. We cut down expenses as much as we can, but it is impossible to make ends meet. We began to sell things, trinkets and so on, without interfering with his beloved collection. There was very little to sell, since Father had always spent whatever he could scrape together upon woodcuts, copper-plate engravings, and the like. The collector's mania! Well, at length it was a question whether we were to touch the collection or let him starve. We didn't ask permission. What would have been the use? He hasn't the ghost of a notion how hard food is to come by, at any price; has never heard that Germany was defeated and surrendered Alsace-Lorraine. We don't read him items of that sort from the newspaper!

"The first piece we sold was a very valuable one, a Rembrandt etching, and the dealer paid us a long price, a good many thousand marks. We thought it would last us for years. But you know how money was melting away in 1922 and 1923. After we had provided for our immediate needs, we put the rest in a bank. In two months it was gone! We had to sell another engraving, and then another. That was during the worst days of inflation, and each time the dealer delayed settlement until the price was not worth a tenth or a hundredth of what he had promised to pay. We tried auction-rooms, and were cheated there too, though the bids were raised by millions. The million- or milliard-mark notes were waste-paper by the time we got them. The collection was scattered to provide daily bread, and little of that.

"That was why Mother was so much alarmed when you turned up today. Directly the portfolios are opened, our pious fraud will be disclosed. He knows each item by touch. You see, every print we disposed of was immediately replaced by a sheet of blank cartridge-paper of the same size and thickness, so that he would notice no difference when he handled it. Feeling them one by one, and counting them, he derives almost as much pleasure as if he could actually see them. He never tries to show them to anyone here, where there is no connoisseur, no one worthy to look at them; but he loves each of them so ardently that I think his heart would break if he knew they had been dispersed. The last time he asked someone to look at them, it was the curator of the copper-plate engravings in Dresden, who died years ago.

"I beseech you"—her voice broke—"not to shatter his illusion, not to undermine his faith, that the treasures he will describe to you are there for the seeing. He would not survive the knowledge of their loss. Perhaps we have wronged him; yet what could we do? One must live. Orphaned children are more valuable than old prints. Besides, it has been life and happiness to him to spend three hours every afternoon going through his imaginary collection, and talking to each specimen as if it were a friend. Today may be the most enthralling experience since his sight failed. How he has longed for the chance of exhibiting his treasures to an expert! If you will lend yourself to the deception. . . . "

In my cold recital, I cannot convey to you how poignant was this appeal. I have seen many a sordid transaction in my business career; have had to look on supinely while persons ruined by inflation have been diddled out of cherished heirlooms which they were compelled to sacrifice for a crust. But my heart has not been utterly calloused, and this tale touched me to the quick. I need hardly tell you that I promised to play up.

We went to her house together. On the way I was grieved (though not surprised) to learn for what preposterously small amounts these ignorant though kind-hearted women had parted with prints many of which were extremely valuable and some of them unique. This confirmed my resolve to give all the help in my power. As we mounted the stairs we heard a jovial shout: "Come in! Come in!" With the keen hearing of the blind, he had recognized the footsteps for which he had been eagerly waiting.

"Franz usually takes a siesta after dinner, but excitement kept him awake today," said the old woman with a smile as she let us in. A glance at her daughter showed her that all was well. The stack of portfolios was on the table. The blind collector seized me by the arm and thrust me into a chair which was placed ready for me.

"Let's begin at once. There's a lot to see, and time presses. The first portfolio contains Dürers. Nearly a full set, and you'll think each cut finer than the others. Magnificent specimens. Judge for yourself."

He opened the portfolio as he spoke, saying:

"We start with the Apocalypse series, of course."

Then, tenderly, delicately (as one handles fragile and precious objects), he picked up the first of the blank sheets of cartridge-paper and held it admiringly before my sighted eyes and his blind ones. So enthusiastic was his gaze that it was difficult to believe he could not see. Though I knew it to be fancy, I found it difficult to doubt that there was a glow of recognition in the wrinkled visage.

"Have you ever come across a finer print? How sharp the impression. Every detail crystal-clear. I compared mine with the one at Dresden; a good one, no doubt, but 'fuzzy' in contrast with the specimen you are looking at. Then I have the whole pedigree."

He turned the sheet over and pointed at the back so convincingly that involuntarily I leaned forward to read the non-existent inscriptions.

"The stamp of the Nagler collection, followed by those of Remy and Esdaille. My famous predecessors never thought that their treasure would come to roost in this little room."

I shuddered as the unsuspecting enthusiast extolled the blank sheet of paper; my flesh crept when he placed a fingernail on the exact spot where the alleged imprints had been made·by long-dead collectors. It was as ghostly as if the disembodied spirits of the men he named had risen from the tomb. My tongue clave to the roof of my mouth—until once more I caught sight of the distraught countenance of Kronfeld's wife and daughter. Then I pulled myself together and resumed my role. With forced heartiness, I exclaimed:

"Certainly you are right. This specimen is peerless."

He swelled with triumph.

"But that's nothing," he went on. "Look at these two, the *Melancholia,* and the illuminated print of the *Passion.* The latter, beyond question, has no equal. The freshness of the tints! Your colleagues in Berlin and the custodians of the public galleries would turn green with envy at the sight."

I will not bore you with details. Thus it went on, a paean, for more than two hours, as he ransacked portfolio after portfolio. An eerie business to watch the handling of these two or three hundred blanks, to chime in at appropriate moments with praise of merits which for the blind collector were so eminently real that again and again (this was my salvation) his faith kindled my own.

Once only did disaster loom. He was "showing" me a first proof of Rembrandt's *Antiope,* which must have been of inestimable value and which had doubtless been sold for a song. Again he dilated on the sharpness of the print, but as he passed his fingers lightly over it the sensitive tips missed some familiar indentation. His face clouded, his mouth trembled, and he said:

"Surely, surely it's the *Antiope?* No one touches the woodcuts and etchings but myself. How can it have got misplaced?"

"Of course it's the *Antiope,* Herr Kronfeld," I said, hastening to take the "print" from his hand and to expatiate upon various details which my own remembrance enabled me to conjure up upon the blank surface.

His bewilderment faded. The more I praised, the more gratified he became, until at last he said exultantly to the two women:

"Here's a man who knows what's what! You have been inclined to grumble at my 'squandering' money upon the collection. It's true that for half a century and more I denied myself beer, wine, tobacco, travelling, visits to the theatre, books, devoting all I could spare to these purchases you have despised. Well, Herr Rackner confirms my judgment. When I am dead and gone, you'll be richer than anyone in the town, as wealthy as the wealthiest folk in Dresden, and you'll have good reason for congratulating yourself on my 'craze.' But so long as I'm alive, the collection must be kept together. After I've been boxed and buried, this expert or another will help you to sell. You'll have to, since my pension dies with me."

As he spoke, his fingers caressed the despoiled portfolios. It was horrible and touching. Not for years, not since 1914, had I witnessed an expression of such unmitigated happiness on the face of a German. His wife and daughter watched him with tear-dimmed eyes, yet ecstatically, like those women of old who—affrighted and rapturous—found the stone rolled away and the sepulchre empty in the garden outside the wall of Jerusalem. But the man could not have enough of my appreciation. He went on from portfolio to portfolio, from "print" to "print," drinking in my words, until, outwearied, I was glad when the lying blanks were replaced in their cases and room was made to serve coffee on the table.

My host, far from being tired, looked rejuvenated. He had story after story to tell concerning the way he had chanced upon his multifarious treasures, wanting, in this connexion, to take out each relevant piece once more. He grew peevish when I insisted, when his wife and daughter insisted, that I should miss my train if he delayed me any longer. . . .

In the end he was reconciled to my going, and we said good-bye. His voice mellowed; he took both my hands in his and fondled them with the tactile appreciation of the blind.

"Your visit has given me immense pleasure," he said with a quaver in his voice. "What a joy to have been able at long last to show my collection to one competent to appreciate it. I can do something to prove my gratitude, to make your visit to a blind old man worth while. A codicil to my will shall stipulate that your firm, whose probity everyone knows, will be entrusted with the auctioning of my collection."

He laid a hand lovingly upon the pile of worthless portfolios.

"Promise me they shall have a handsome catalogue. I could ask no better monument."

I glanced at the two women, who were exercising the utmost control, fearful lest the sound of their trembling should reach his keen ears. I promised the impossible, and he pressed my hand in response.

Wife and daughter accompanied me to the door. They did not venture to speak, but tears were flowing down their cheeks. I myself was in little better case. An art-dealer, I had come in search of bargains. Instead, as events turned out, I had been a sort of angel of good-luck, lying like a trooper in order to assist in a fraud which kept an old man happy. Ashamed of lying, I was glad that I had lied. At any rate I had aroused an ecstacy which seems foreign to this period of sorrow and gloom.

As I stepped forth into the street, I heard a window open, and my name called. Though the old fellow could not see me, he knew in which direction I should walk, and his sightless eyes were turned thither. He leaned out so far that his anxious relatives put their arms round him lest he should fall. Waving a handkerchief, he shouted:

"A pleasant journey to you, Herr Rackner."

His voice rang like a boy's. Never shall I forget that cheerful face, which contrasted so grimly with the careworn aspect of the passers-by in the street. The illusion I had helped to sustain made life good for him. Was it not Goethe who said:

"Collectors are happy creatures"?

S. WILLIAM HALPERIN
The Great Depression

In *Germany Tried Democracy* S. William Halperin describes the depression which hit Germany in 1930. The German people took great pride in having, through heroic efforts, overcome the effects of the inflation of 1923. When the Great Depression struck Germany, the people began to experience the same conditions which had been so disastrous only seven years earlier. This new catastrophe caused most Germans to turn to the extreme left wing or right wing political movements. The depression proved to be the immediate event most responsible for Nazi popularity.

GERMANY'S FINANCIAL DIFFICULTIES at this moment were already grave enough to cause widespread and mounting concern. But they became immeasurably worse as a result of developments far from her own borders. Heralded by the crash of October, 1929, on the New York Stock Exchange, an economic depression of record-shattering proportions began to engulf the world. It spread with irresistible momentum. Its lightning struck everywhere, but nowhere more swiftly than in highly industrialized countries like the United States, Great Britain and Germany. Upon the latter the depression descended early and with terrific impact. By the spring of 1930, all the symptoms of economic malaise were in evidence. The tempo of industry, which had been so phenomenal during the past few years, slackened markedly. Prices and wages began to decline. Unemployment continued to increase. Bankruptcies and fore-closures became everyday occurrences. The biggest blow of all was the drying up of Germany's sources of foreign credit. Her prosperity from 1925 to 1929 was in large measure the artificial result of huge loans from abroad. When no more loans were forthcoming, the props were literally taken from under the business boom, which came down like a house of cards. But this was only one, although the biggest factor. High tariff barriers all over the world were keeping German exports out. The United States, Great Britain, and France were cutting into Germany's markets. Russia, which had been so lucrative a preserve for German industry before 1914, was still largely inaccessible. Rationalization had reduced the demand for labor, and the worldwide fall of agricultural prices was wiping out the recent gains of the peasantry. The net result was a sharply decreased purchasing power at home.

Everybody suffered. Wage earners, as usual, were hard hit. The lucky ones were able to keep their jobs at greatly reduced rates of pay. The rest found themselves dependent on a slender dole or completely destitute. The streets were cluttered with hungry men seeking employment, while at home their families clamored for food as the grip of starvation closed relentlessly around them. Equally desperate was the plight of the lower middle class: petty shop-keepers, modest rentiers, clerks, intellectuals, professional people. The workers at least had their trade unions to fight for them; they had unemployment insurance to cushion the first impact of adversity. But the people just above them in the social hierarchy were completely defenseless because they were unorganized. They had nothing to fall back on when misfortune overtook them. They were full of class pride, and poverty for them was more than material want; it was a stigma, a brand; it meant the loss not only of status but of self-respect. Before their eyes there unfolded the horrible prospect of steady degradation, with the gutter as the final resting place. *Little Man, What Now?* Hans Fallada's moving novel about humble German folk who fought a losing battle against economic adversity, tells a story that makes the spread of Nazism all too understandable. The misfortunes that befell Fallada's characters were typical of what happened to millions of honest, self-respecting and hard-working Germans who wanted only a modest livelihood to sustain themselves and their families but who found all the cards stacked against them.

In their desperation, the victims of the depression turned not only upon themselves but upon those more fortunate than they. Little shop-keepers tearfully liquidating their business cursed the ever flourishing department stores. People who saw the modest savings of a lifetime dwindle and disappear learned to hate their affluent neighbors. Jobless clerks envied their bosses. Hordes of university graduates found the doors of opportunity securely closed against them and thought malevolently about those on the inside. Even before the depression, Germany had had far too many doctors and lawyers. When hard times came along, marginal practitioners went under. For the more embittered of these there was no solace save the hope of dragging others down with them. The peasants were having a rough time of it, too, but they knew from past experience that their pleas for assistance would go unheeded. Staggering under the burden of taxation, working with implements all too often purchased with borrowed money, and faced with the possibility of losing even their modest homesteads as a result of the calamitous toboggan of farm prices, they found little to sustain them in this dark hour and even less to look forward to. Never before, in time of peace, had the mass of Germans suffered so.

The depression staggered the republic. It unleashed forces which the Nazis harnessed for their own purposes. They eventually created a totalitarian dictatorship in Germany. Then they turned the world topsy-turvy. But it all began with the depression. The key to Hitler's rise lies there. . . .

*   *   *

The government now figured [1930] on an average of 1,600,000 recipients of unemployment benefits and 400,000 recipients of poor relief (this left about a million jobless unaccounted for), thus making a total of two million persons as against 1,400,000, the number hitherto reckoned with. At the beginning of May, 1930, the deficit in the unemployment insurance fund stood at 450 million marks. An additional 150 million marks had to be found for the poor relief fund. The revenues earmarked for both these funds fell far below expectations. Another complication was the necessity of setting aside 100 million marks for the purpose of financing a public works program. In its effort to balance the budget, the government was prepared to resort to drastic measures. It proposed emergency levies on bachelors, individuals with fixed salaries and businessmen who earned fees as directors of corporations. It called for an increase of one per cent (which meant raising the rate from three and one-half to four and one-half per cent) in unemployment insurance premiums.

HANS FALLADA
Little Man, What Now?

Hans Fallada's *Little Man, What Now?* is a moving account of the
suffering experienced by millions of hard-working Germans. Their
hopeless struggle against economic adversity makes the success of
Nazism all too understandable. Perhaps the most significant aspect of
the story, however, is the evidence of the psychic damage experienced
through loss of position and place.

BUT NO: life went on. Everything did. It was November, in the
following year, fourteen months since Pinneberg had left his work at
Mandel's. A dark, cold, damp November, all very well when the roof
is sound. The roof of their hut was sound, Pinneberg had given it a
fresh coating of tar a month before. He was now awake, the
illuminated dial of the alarm clock showed a quarter to five.
Pinneberg listened to the November rain hissing and rattling on the
timber roof. It will keep the rain out, he thought. I've fixed it
properly. The rain can't hurt us, anyway.

He was just about to turn round comfortably and go to sleep
again, when it suddenly occurred to him that he had been awakened
by a noise: the garden gate had clicked. Krymna would be knocking
in a moment. Pinneberg took Bunny's arm as she lay beside him in
the narrw iron bed and tried to waken her gently. She started up and
said, "What's the matter?"

Bunny had lost her joyful awakening of old days; if she was
awakened at an unusual time, it was always for bad news.

"Don't talk too loud," whispered Pinneberg. "You'll wake the
baby. It isn't five o'clock yet."

"What is it?" asked Bunny again, rather impatiently.

"Krymna's coming," whispered Pinneberg. "Shall I go with him?"

"No, no, no," said Bunny passionately. "That's settled, do you
hear? I'll have no thieving."

"But . . . " pleaded Pinneberg.

There was a knock outside. A voice called: "Pinneberg!" and
"Are you coming, Pinneberg?"

Pinneberg jumped up and for a moment stood in doubt.

"So . . . " he began and listened.

Bunny did not answer.

"Pinneberg! Come out, you old rascal!" came the voice once more.

Pinneberg felt his way in the darkness on to the little porch, through the glass panes he could see the dark outline of the other man's form.

"At last! Coming or not?"

"I . . . " cried Pinneberg through the door, "I should like to."

"Then you aren't?"

"Look here, Krymna, I would but my wife—you know how women are."

"Then you aren't," shouted Krymna from without. "Okay. We'll go alone."

Pinneberg looked after him. He could recognize Krymna's squat figure against the slightly lighter sky. The garden door slammed and Krymna was swallowed up by the night.

Pinneberg sighed once more. He was very cold, standing there in his shirt, and he knew he ought to go in. But there he stood and stared. From within the baby called out: "Da-Da! Ma-Ma!"

Softly Pinneberg felt his way back into the room. "The baby must sleep," he said; "he must get a bit more sleep." The child was breathing deeply, his father heard him lying in his bed. "Dolly," he whispered; "Dolly!"

Pinneberg groped about the room in the darkness, looking for the india rubber doll. The child had to have it in his hand before he would fall asleep. He found the doll. "Here's dolly, darling; hold him tight. And now go to sleep." The child emitted a gurgle of satisfaction and happiness and was soon asleep.

Pinneberg also went back to bed, and as he was so cold, he tried to avoid any contact with Bunny, not wishing to alarm her.

There he lay, unsleeping, indeed it was then too late for that to matter much. He thought of all manner of things: whether Krymna was very angry with him for refusing to go out and "look for" wood, and whether Krymna could do him much harm in the neighborhood. Then he wondered how they were going to afford briquettes, now that they would have no wood. He reflected that he would have to go to town that day to draw the dole. And then that he must also call on Puttbreese, to pay him six marks. The old man did not want the money, he would only spend it on drink; it made Pinneberg wild to think of the way people wasted the money that others so sorely needed. Pinneberg then reflected that Heilbutt must also be paid his ten marks, and this would absorb all the dole. How he was going to get food and fuel for the coming week, heaven alone knew—or perhaps didn't.

And so it went on, for weeks and weeks, months and months. That was what was so ghastly—it just went on and on. Had he ever thought that it would end? The appalling thing was that it always went on, on and on, just the same . . . future there was none. . . .

Pinneberg dressed the baby. Then he said, turning towards the bed; "Time to get up, Bunny."

"Yes," said she obediently, and began to dress. "What did Krymna say?"

"Oh, nothing, he was sore."

"I don't care. I won't have you mixed up with that sort of thing."

"Well," said Pinneberg cautiously. "It's quite safe, you know. There are always about six or eight of them go out to get wood. So the foresters don't interfere."

"Never mind," said Bunny. "We just don't do that sort of thing."

"And how are we going to get the money for the coal?"

"I've got another whole day's darning at the Krämers' today. That makes three marks. And tomorrow I may get a day's mending at the Rechlins'. That's another three marks. And the next week I've got three days' work fixed up already. I'm doing well here."

The room seemed to brighten as she spoke, the air was sweeter for her presence.

"It's such tiring work," he said, "Nine hours darning, for so little money."

"But you must figure in the food," she said. "I get a lot to eat at the Krämers'. I'll be able to bring some back for you in the evening."

"You must eat your own food," said Pinneberg.

"But I get such a lot at the Krämers'," said Bunny once more.

Day had come. The sun had risen. He blew out the lamp, they sat down to their coffee. The baby sat sometimes on his father's knee and sometimes on his mother's. He drank his milk, and ate his bread, and his eyes glowed with pleasure in the new day.

"If you go to town today," said Bunny, "you might bring back a quarter pound of butter for him. I don't think all this margerine is doing him any good. He's cutting so many teeth."

"Oh, and I must take Puttbreese his six marks today."

"Yes, you must. Don't forget."

"And Heilbutt must have his ten marks. The day after tomorrow is the first of the month."

"Right," said Bunny.

"That finishes the dole money. I've got just enough for fares."

"I can give you another five marks," said Bunny. "I get three more today. So you can buy the butter, and you might see if you can get some bananas at five pfennigs on the Alex—the robbers charge fifteen here. As if anyone would pay such a price!"

"I will," he said. "Try not to be too late, I don't like the boy being left alone so long."

"I'll see what I can do. I imagine I can be back by half-past five. I suppose you'll start about one?"

"Yes," he said. "At two I have to be at the Labor Office."

"It'll be all right," she said. "It's not nice, I know, to leave the baby alone in the hut. But nothing has ever happened."

"No, and won't until it does."

"You mustn't talk like that," said she. "Why should we be always out of luck? Now I've got all this mending and darning to do, we aren't getting on so bad."

"No," he said slowly. "No, of course not."

"Oh my dear," she cried. "Things will improve one of these days, I'm sure they will. Keep your chin up."

"I didn't marry," he said doggedly, "for you to keep me. . . . "

Pinneberg reflected on all this as he sat in his train . . . and stared at his ticket. The ticket was yellow, and cost fifty pfennigs; the return also cost fifty pfennigs, and as Pinneberg had to call at the Labor Exchange twice a week, out of his eighteen marks' unemployed pay, two marks went on fares. This expense always made Pinneberg furious.

There were indeed cheap workman's tickets but to get them Pinneberg had to live where he was really living, and that he could not do. There was also a Labor Exchange near-by, where he could get his card stamped without having to waste money on fares, but for the same reason he could not use it: he did not officially live in the hut. For the purpose of the Labor Exchange Pinneberg lived in Puttbreese's establishment, today, tomorrow, and for all eternity, whether he could pay the rent or not.

There was nothing to be done. The Pinnebergs still lived officially in Berlin in Puttbreese's house, and Pinneberg had to travel to town twice each week to draw his money. And every two weeks he had to visit the detested Puttbreese and pay him six marks off his arrears of rent.

When Pinneberg had been sitting for an hour or so in the train, he piled up all his afflictions in his mind and they flared up into quite a pretty little blaze of anger, hatred and bitterness. But it did not last. When he came to push his way through the Labor Exchange in the gray monotonous stream of his fellows—all kinds of faces and all kinds of clothes, but in all their hearts the same conflict, the same misery, the same bitterness . . . . Oh, what was the use? Why get excited? Tens of thousands were worse off than he, tens of thousands had no such wife to back them up, and they had, not one child, but half a dozen. Move on, Pinneberg, my man, draw your money and clear out. . . .

Pinneberg stopped in front of a dress-shop window in which there was a large mirror. He looked himself up and down: no, not a pleasant sight. His light gray trousers were tar-stained from his labors on the hut roof, his overcoat was worn and faded, his shoes were in their last stages, . . . it was stupid to wear a collar with such clothes. He was just a broken-down creature without a job, anyone could see that twenty yards away. Pinneberg grabbed at his collar, tore it off, and stuffed it and his necktie into his coat-pocket. He did not now look very different, indeed he could hardly have looked much worse. . . .

A police car suddenly dashed past. So there had been another row with the Nazis or the Communists—the fellows had some courage left. He wished he still took a newspaper—you didn't know what was going on. All might be in perfect order in the land of Germany, he noticed nothing in his country hut. Well, well, if things were in such good shape, he would have noticed.

Thus he mused as he walked; it was a cheerless way of passing the time, but what else was a man to do in a city where he was presumably expected to stay home and brood over his troubles. . . .

In former days Pinneberg had often walked down the Friedrichstrasse, it was an old haunt of his and he noticed how many more girls there were. For some time now, of course, they had not all been regulars, there had been much unfair competition in late years; even eighteen months ago he had heard in the shop that many wives of men out of work had gone on the streets to earn a few marks.

It was true—indeed it was obvious; many of them were so utterly without attraction or prospects or success, or, if they had any looks, greed, and greed for money, was written on their faces.

Pinneberg thought of Bunny and the boy. "We aren't so bad off," Bunny would often say. She was certainly right.

There still seemed a certain amount of excitement among the police, all the patrols were doubled, and every minute or two he passed a pair of officers parading the pavement. Pinneberg had nothing against the police; but he could not help feeling that they looked irritatingly well-fed and clothed, and behaved, too, in rather a provocative way. They walked among the public like teachers among school-children during the play interval: —Behave properly, or—!

Well, let them be.

For the fourth time Pinneberg was pacing that section of the Friedrichstrasse that lies between the Leipziger and the Linden. He could not go home, he simply revolted at the thought. When he got home, everything was at a dead end, life flickered into a dim and hopeless distance. But here something still might happen. It was true that the girls did not look at him; a man with so threadbare a coat, such dirty trousers and without a collar did not exist for the girls on the Friedrichstrasse. If he wanted anything of that kind, he had better go along to the Schlesischer; there they did not mind appearances so long as the man could pay. But did he want a girl?

Perhaps he did, he was not sure, he thought no more of the matter. He just wanted to tell some human being what his life had once been, the smart suits he had had, and talk about—

He had entirely forgotten the boy's butter and bananas, it was now nine o'clock and all the shops would be shut! Pinneberg was furious with himself, and even more sorry than angry; he could not go home empty-handed, what would Bunny think of him? Perhaps he could get something at the side-door of a shop. There was a great grocer's shop, radiantly illuminated. Pinneberg flattened his nose against the window. Pherhaps there was still someone about. He must get that butter and bananas!

A voice behind him said in a low tone: "Move on please!"

Pinneberg started—he was really quite frightened. A policeman stood beside him.

Was the man speaking to him?

"Move on there, do you hear?" said the policeman, loudly now. There were other people standing at the shop-window, well-dressed people, but to them the policeman had undoubtedly not addressed himself.He meant Pinneberg.

"What? But why—? Can't I—?"

He stammered; he simply did not understand.

"Are you going?" asked the policeman. "Or shall I—?"

The loop of his rubber club was slipped around his wrist, and he raised the weapon slightly.

Everyone stared at Pinneberg. Some passers-by had stopped, a little crowd began to collect. The people looked on expectantly, they took no sides in the matter; on the previous day shop-windows had been broken on the Friedrich and the Leipziger.

The policeman had dark eyebrows, bright resolute eyes, a straight nose, red cheeks, and an energetic moustache.

"Well?" said the policeman calmly.

Pinneberg tried to speak; Pinneberg looked at the policeman; his lips quivered, and he looked at the bystanders. A little group was standing round the window, well-dressed people, respectable people, people who earned money.

But in the mirror of the window still stood a lone figure, a pale phantom, collarless, clad in a shabby ulster and tar-smeared trousers.

Suddenly Pinneberg understood everything; in the presence of this policeman, these respectable persons, this gleaming window, he understood that he was outside it all, that he no longer belonged here and that he was rightly chased away; he had slipped into the abyss, and was engulfed. Order and cleanliness; they were of the past. So too were work and safe subsistence. And past too were progress and hope. Poverty was not merely misery, poverty was an offence, poverty was evil, poverty meant that a man was suspect.

"Do you want one on the bean?" asked the policeman.

Pinneberg obeyed; he was aware of nothing but a longing to hurry to the Friedrichstrasse station and catch his train and get back to Bunny.

Pinneberg was conscious of a blow on his shoulder, not a heavy blow, but just enough to land him in the gutter.

"Beat it!" said the policeman. "And be quick about it!"

Pinneberg went; he shuffled along in the gutter close to the curb and thought of a great many things, of fires and bombs and street shooting and how Bunny and the baby were done for: it was all over . . . but really his mind was vacant.

Pinneberg came to the junction of the Jägerstrasse and the

Friedrichstrasse. He wanted to cross to the railway station, and so get home to Bunny and the baby. He began to feel himself a man again. The policeman gave him a push. "That's your way, young fellow." He pointed down the Jägerstrasse.

Once more Pinneberg tried to mutiny; he had to catch his train. "But I must . . . " he said.

"That's your way, I tell you, " repeated the officer, and pushed him into the Jägerstrasse. "Get a move on." And he gave Pinneberg an emphatic shove in the desired direction.

Pinneberg began to run; he ran very fast, he realized the men were no longer following him, but he did not dare look around. He ran along the roadway into the night, straight ahead, into the darkness, into the night that was not black enough to cover him.

After a long time he slackened his step. He stopped and looked around. No one. Nothing. No police. Cautiously he raised one foot and placed it on the pavement. Then the other. He stood no longer in the roadway, he stood upon the pavement.

Then Pinneberg went on, step by step, through the city of Berlin. But it was nowhere very dark, and it was very difficult to slip past the policemen. . . .

The sky was clear and starry and there was a light frost. Among all the huts, so far as she could see, not a light was visible; only behind her, in the window of their own hut, shown the soft reddish glow of the oil lamp.

There Bunny stood, the baby slept—was she waiting? What was she waiting for? The last train was through, he could not get back until tomorrow morning, he had gone off on a spree—one more affliction that she had not been spared. She had been spared nothing. She could go to bed and sleep. Or lie awake. It didn't matter.

Bunny did not go in. She stood there; in that silent night there was something that made her heart uneasy. Up yonder the familiar stars glittered in the chill air. The bushes in the garden and in the neighboring garden were crude compact masses of blackness, and the next hut stood like a great dark beast.

No wind, not a sound, nothing; far away in the distance rumbled a train. There in that garden the silence was tense and still, and Bunny knew she was not alone. Someone was standing in the darkness, just as she was, motionless. Did he breathe? No, not a breath. And yet there was someone there.

There was an elderbush, there was another. Since when had there been something between them?

Bunny took a step forward, her heart was hammering, she said very quietly: "Darling, is that you?"

The bush, the bush that she had never noticed, was silent. Then it moved very slowly. . . .

Pinneberg did not answer.

For a while they stood silent; his face was not visible and yet, coming from that silent figure that confronted her, she was conscious of a waft of peril, something still darker than the night, something more menacing than this strange rigidity of the man she knew so well.

Bunny stood still, then she said lightly: "Shall we go in? I'm feeling cold."

He did not answer.

Something had happened. It was not that he'd been drinking, or at least it was not only that—he had perhaps been drinking too. Something else had happened, something worse.

There stood her husband, the boy whom she so loved, in the darkness, like a wounded beast not daring to come into the light. They had got him down at last. . . .

Once more they stood for a while: on the road beneath them, Bunny could hear a car, far away; then the hum of it approached, grew louder, and then gradually faded into silence. What should she say? If only he would speak!

"I've been doing some mending at the Krämers' today, you know."

He did not answer.

"At least—I didn't do any darning. She had a piece of material, and I cut out a house frock and made it up for her. She was very pleased; she's going to let me have her old sewing machine cheap and recommend me to all her friends. I get eight marks for making a dress, and sometimes ten."

She waited. She waited quite a while. Then she said cautiously: "Maybe we'll be making good money soon; our troubles may be over."

He moved slightly; then he again stood still and was silent.

Bunny waited, her heart was heavy within her, she felt very cold. She had no more words of comfort. She could do no more. Why should she struggle further? For what? He might as well have gone out to steal wood with the rest.

Once more she gazed up at the myriad stars. The heavens were still and solemn, but strange and vast and very far away. She said:

"The boy kept asking for you all afternoon."

No answer.

"Oh my darling!" she cried. "What is it? Do say just one word to your Bunny. Am I nothing to you any more? Are we—just alone?"

It was no good. He came no nearer, he said nothing; he seemed farther and farther away.

The cold had risen to Bunny's heart; it gripped her until she was chilled through and through. Behind her shone the warm red light of the hut window, where the baby was asleep. Alas, children depart also, they are ours only for a while—six years? Ten years? We are all of us alone.

She turned towards the red glow, she must go in—what else could she do?

Behind her a voie called from far away: "Bunny!"

She went on; it was no use, she went on.

"Bunny!"

She went on. There was the hut, there was the door, one step more and her hand was on the latch.

She felt herself held fast, he was gripping her, he sobbed, he stammered out: "Oh Bunny, do you know what they did to me? The police . . . they shoved me off the pavement . . . they chased me away. How can I ever look anybody in the face again!"

Suddenly the cold had gone, an infinite green wave raised her up, and him with her. They slid onwards, and the twinkling stars came very near. She whispered: "You can always look at me. Always and always. You're here with me and we're together."

The wave rose and rose. They lay on the sea-shore by night between Lensahn and Weik, once more the stars were close above their heads. The wave rose higher and higher, from the polluted earth towards the stars.

Then they both went into the hut where the baby lay asleep.

III Hitler Provides Answers

In the previous section emphasis was placed on the problems faced by the Weimar Republic and the German people. In this section the selections were chosen to show that the solutions which Hitler proposed to those problems found response in every element of the German people.

Hitler discovered very early in his political career that he had a powerful impact on his audience when he spoke. He had a charismatic appeal which is uniquely characteristc of the twentieth century, and is associated particularly with totalitarian movements. His instinctive ability to sense the mood of a crowd and to pitch his address to that mood spread his fame and gained supporters with every speech. But Hitler added a mastery of propaganda techniques which enabled him to get support from socialists and anti-socialists, peasants and landlords, laborers and capitalists, with each group convinced that he was speaking only to them.

An inner circle of disciples developed an unquestioning loyalty and helped convert the German people to the new cult. Support from major leaders of the army, business community, and even royalty and nobility lent respectability to his virulent attacks against Jews, democrats, communists, supporters of the existing government—in short, everyone who was not a Nazi.

As the economic crisis deepened in 1930 and following, and the Weimar political parties failed to provide the answers to the Republic's problems, increasing numbers of voters turned to the support of Hitler at the polls. Through the calculated use of violence and with the connivance of those responsible for protecting the Republic, the Nazis became the largest single party in the state, and Hitler accepted appointment as Chancellor.

The Party Program

Even before Hitler gained control of the Nazi Party, he had helped Gottfried Feder write the Twenty-Five Points of the German Workers' Party. This program contained many of the solutions which Hitler proposed for Germany's problems, and at the same time served as the basis for much of his best propaganda efforts.

THE PROGRAM of the German Workers' Party is limited as to period. The leaders have no intention, once the aims announced in it have been achieved, of setting up fresh ones, merely in order to increase the discontent of the masses artificially, and so ensure the continued existence of the party.

1. We demand the union of all Germans to form a Great Germany on the basis of the right of self-determination enjoyed by nations.

2. We demand equality of rights for the German people in its dealings with other nations, and abolition of the peace treaties of Versailles and Saint-Germain.

3. We demand land and territory (colonies) for the nourishment of our people and for settling our excess population.

4. None but members of the nation may be citizens of the state. None but those of German blood, whatever their creed, may be members of the nation. No Jew, therefore, may be a member of the nation.

5. Anyone who is not a citizen of the state may live in Germany only as a guest and must be regarded as being subject to foreign laws.

6. The right of voting on the leadership and legislation is to be enjoyed by the state alone. We demand therefore that all official appointments, of whatever kind, whether in the Reich, in the country, or in the smaller localities, shall be granted to citizens of the state alone. We oppose the corrupting custom of Parliament of filling posts merely with a view to party considerations, and without reference to character or capacity.

7. We demand that the state shall make it its first duty to promote the industry and livelihood of citizens of the state. If it is not possible to nourish the entire population of the state, foreign

From Raymond E. Murphy, ed., *National Socialism,* U.S. Department of State, Publication 1864 (Washington, 1943), pp. 222-25.

nationals (non-citizens of the state) must be excluded from the Reich.

8. All non-German immigration must be prevented. . . .

9. All citizens of the state shall be equal as regards rights and duties.

10. It must be the first duty of each citizen of the state to work with his mind or with his body. The activities of the individual may not clash with the interests of the whole, but must proceed within the frame of the community and be for the general good.

We demand therefore:

11. Abolition of incomes unearned by work.

12. In view of the enormous sacrifice of life and property demanded of a nation by every war, personal enrichment due to a war must be regarded as a crime against the nation. We demand therefore ruthless confiscation of all war gains.

13. We demand nationalization of all businesses (trusts). . . .

14. We demand that the profits from wholesale trade shall be shared.

15. We demand extensive development of provision for old age.

16. We demand creation and maintenance of a healthy middle class, immediate communalization of wholesale business premises, and their lease at a cheap rate to small traders, and that extreme consideration shall be shown to all small purveyors to the state, district authorities, and smaller localities.

17. We demand land reform suitable to our national requirements. . . .

18. We demand ruthless prosecution of those whose activities are injurious to the common interest. Sordid criminals against the nation, usurers, profiteers, etc., must be punished with death, whatever their creed or race.

19. We demand that the Roman Law, which serves the materialistic world order, shall be replaced by a legal system for all Germany.

20. With the aim of opening to every capable and industrious German the possibility of higher education and of thus obtaining advancement, the state must consider a thorough reconstruction of our national system of education. . . .

21. The state must see to raising the standard of health in the nation by protecting mothers and infants, prohibiting child labor, increasing bodily efficiency by obligatory gymnastics and sports laid down by law, and by extensive support of clubs engaged in the bodily development of the young.

22. We demand abolition of a paid army and formation of a national army.

23. We demand legal warfare against conscious political lying and its dissemination in the press. In order to facilitate creation of a German national press we demand:

a) that all editors of newspapers and their assistants, employing the German language, must be members of the nation;

b) that special permission from the state shall be necessary before non-German newspapers may appear. These are not necessarily printed in the German language;

c) that non-Germans shall be prohibited by law from participation financially in or influencing German newspapers. . . .

It must be forbidden to publish papers which do not conduce to the national welfare. We demand legal prosecution of all tendencies in art and literature of a kind likely to disintegrate our life as a nation, and the suppression of institutions which militate against the requirements above-mentioned.

24. We demand liberty for all religious denominations in the state, so far as they are not a danger to it and do not militate against the moral feelings of the German race.

The party, as such, stands for positive Christianity, but does not bind itself in the matter of creed to any particular confession. It combats the Jewish-materialist spirit within us and without us. . . .

25. That all the foregoing may be realized we demand the creation of a strong central power of the state. Unquestioned authority of the politically centralized Parliament over the entire Reich and its organizations; and formation of chambers for classes and occupations for the purpose of carrying out the general laws promulgated by the Reich in the various states of the confederation.

The leaders of the party swear to go straight forward—if necessary to sacrifice their lives—in securing fulfillment of the foregoing points.

ADOLF HITLER
The Role of the Party

As early as 1923 Adolf Hitler had discovered the power of his voice over the masses of the German people. The following speech (August 1, 1923) illustrates the technique he used to gain support from the dissatisfied people by a bitter denunciation of the Republic and castigation of its founders and leaders. Already he was making use of anti-semitism, but his chief points at this early date were concerned with German nationalism.

OUR MOVEMENT is opposed with the cry 'The Republic is in danger!' Your Republic of the 9th of November? In very truth it is: the November-Republic is in danger! How long, think you, can you maintain this 'State'? . . . The hour will come when this Republic which denies German history, which has disbanded Germany's old army, which has hauled down and insulted Germany's old flag, the Republic which has become a wrestling-ground for foreign interests—this Republic shall be transformed into a true German 'People's State'—to a true community of all Germans! The State will then for the first time be the German Republic, even if an Emperor or a King should stand at its head! We fight for the State that shall have at its head the greatest cleanliness, the greatest honesty, the proudest strength, the greatest energy. Then upon its external form the people shall decide: it is for the sacred content of that external form that we wage our battle to-day. We had too little faith and love! Rather we should have too much of faith and love: we need an excess of national fanaticism. Ours shall be no State where tolerance reigns. No, we would be intolerant against all who do not wish to be German. You, working men, they are forever lying to you, saying that we are the foes of understanding between peoples. That we are not. Only understanding must not consist in this—that one party gets all the knocks! Two Powers of equal strength can come to an understanding. And precisely because we are nationally minded, for that very reason we have respect for the national feeling of the other peoples. And our national pride does not mean that we scorn other peoples, it means that we respect and love our own

From Norman H. Baynes, ed., *The Speeches of Adolf Hitler, April 1922-August 1939* (2 vols; London: Oxford University Press, 1942), II, 76-79.

people. It is precisely the Internationalists who prevent peoples from coming to understand one another. You are always thrusting yourselves in everywhere and intruding. Thereby you only make yourselves internationally contemptible. One does not beg for a right—one fights for it!

Thus our fight for the cleansing of our domestic life is also a fight for the recovery of the world's respect for the German nation. That is why we have the firm, the immovable faith that victory must be ours!

Our Movement was not formed with any election in view, but in order to spring to the rescue of this people as its last help in the hour of greatest need, at the moment when in fear and despair it sees the approach of the Red Monster. The task of our Movement is still today not to prepare ourselves for any coming election but to prepare for the coming collapse of the Reich, so that when the old trunk falls the young fir-tree may be already standing. . . . Germany can be saved only through action, when through our talking here the bandage has been torn from the eyes of the last of the befooled. It is from our Movement that redemption will come—that to-day is the feeling of millions. That has become almost a new religious faith! And there will be only two possibilities: either Berlin marches and ends up in Munich, or Munich marches and ends up in Berlin! A Bolshevist North Germany and a Nationalist Bavaria cannot exist side by side, and the greatest influence upon the fortunes of the German Reich will be his who shall restore the Reich. On us in Bavaria falls the task to be the cell whence recovery shall come to the rest of the Reich. You will never bring the Bavarian name to any higher honour than on the day when Bavaria will be associated with the liberation of the German nation from its accursed foes within the Reich and with the revival which only that liberation will render possible. Either Germany sinks, and we through our despicable cowardice sink with it, or else we dare to enter on the fight against death and devil and rise up against the fate that has been planned for us. Then we shall see which is the stronger: the spirit of international Jewry or the will of Germany.

JOSEPH GOEBBELS
The Party and the Reichstag

Nazi leaders made no attempt to disguise their contempt for the machinery and institutions of the democratic process. The propaganda chief, Dr. Joseph Goebbels, in an article published in one of the Party newspapers, explained to the rank and file of the Party just why they were to elect their leaders to the Reichstag.

AFTER ALL, we are an anti-parliamentarian party, decline for good reasons the Weimar Consititution and the Republican institutions introduced by it, and are opponents of a counterfeit democracy, which treats intelligent and stupid, diligent and lazy people alike. We see in today's system of majority vote and organized irresponsibility the main cause for our steadily increasing decline. Now, what do we want in the Reichstag?

We go into the Reichstag to supply ourselves at the arsenal of arms of Democracy with its own weapons. We become Deputies of the Reichstag to paralyze the Weimar way of thinking with its own support. If the Democracy is so stupid as to give us free tickets and Deputies' pay for this sham "service," that is its own affair. We will not worry about it. Any lawful means will do if it serves to revolutionize today's conditions.

If we succeed in putting into the different parliaments from sixty to seventy agitators and organizers of our own party, then the State itself will fit out and pay our fighting machine in future. It is an attractive and tantalizing matter, worth while to be tested.

We will also become Parliamentarians once we are in the Parliaments? Is that what we look like? Does any one of you believe that we are going to hobnob right away with Philipp Scheidemann once we march into the plenary meeting of that Illustrious House? Do you consider us such poor revolutionaries that you fear that we would forget our historic mission when faced with a thick red carpet and an air-conditioned dormitory?

Whoever goes into Parliament, perishes in it! Yes, if he goes into Parliament in order to become a Parliamentarian. But if he steps into

From Office of the United States Chief of Counsel for Prosecution of Axis Criminality, *Nazi Conspiracy and Aggression* (8 vols; Washington: United States Government Printing Office, 1946), V, 237-239.

it with the tenacious and dogged intention to continue, with his inborn recklessness, in this place also his unconditional fight against the increasing scoundrelization of our public life, then he will not become a Parliamentarian, but he will remain that what he is: a revolutionary.

Mussolini also went into Parliament. In spite of it, he marched into Rome with his Blackshirts not long afterwards. The Communists also are sitting in the Reichstag. Nobody will be so naive as to believe that they intend to collaborate objectively and positively. And moreover, if we do not succeed this time to gain Parliamentary immunity for our most dangerous men, then they will all sit behind iron bars sooner or later.

They will also sit behind iron bars if they are in possession of Parliamentary immunity? Certainly, namely at that instant in which democracy deems it necessary to get rid of Parliamentary immunity as an act of last desperate self-defense. Then when Democracy is going to slap her own face, and openly sets up the terror of Capitalistic dictatorship, which she exercises normally only clandestinely. But until then much water will flow under the bridge, and in the meantime the champions of our belief, clothed in Parliamentary immunity, will have time and opportunity enough to so enlarge our battlefront that it will not be possible to silence us, and to throttle our public preaching without any noise, as Democracy presumably would like to see it. . . .

If we only wanted to become Deputies in Parliament, then we would not be National Socialists but presumably German Nationalists [*Deutsch Nationale*] or Social Democrats. They have to bestow the most seats in Parliament. One does not have to risk one's life for it, and even *our* brains still suffice for competition with the intellectual luminaries of that party.

We do not beg for votes. We demand conviction, devotion, passion. The vote is only an expedient for us as well as for you. We shall set foot on the marble floor of the Parliament with resounding steps, we shall carry in with us the revolutionary will of the broad masses of the people, out of which we grew, molded by fate and molding fate. We do not give a damn about cooperation in building a stinking dung heap! We come to clean out the dung.

One should not think that Parliamentarism will be our Damascus. We have shown our teeth to our enemies from the platforms of mass meetings and by the giant demonstrations of our own brown guard. We shall show our teeth to them also in the leaden satiety of a Parliamentary plenary meeting.

We do not come either as friends or as neutrals. We come as enemies. Just like the wolf ravages a flock of sheep—thus do we come. Now you are no longer among yourselves. And thus we will not bring you unadulterated joy.

JOHN BRADSHAW HOLT
The Party and Agriculture

The first three states to elect Nazi governments were primarily agricultural. Recognition of the importance of peasant support to the Nazis is evidenced by the promulgation in 1930 of an agrarian program designed to appeal to the depression-hit farmers.

CAUSES OF THESE insufficient returns of farm work are to be sought:

(1) in the present tax policy, which burdens agriculture comparatively heavily. This comes about through the political party interest and because the German parliamentary democracy is really run by a Jewish world financial power which seeks the destruction of German agriculture, for then the German people, especially the workers, will have been sacrificed;

(2) in a competition with foreign agriculture working under better conditions, which because of an anti-agrarian tariff policy is insufficiently shut out;

(3) in the unpermissibly high profits, which the wholesale business of agriculture products by inserting itself between producer and consumer, has been able to derive and which lies for the most part in Jewish hands;

(4) in the usurious prices which the farmers must pay for commercial fertilizer and electricity, generally to Jewish concerns.

From the income of insufficiently repaid farm work it is no longer possible to pay the taxes. The farmer is forced into debt, for which he must pay usurious interest rates. He falls only deeper and deeper into this interest slavery and loses eventually house and farm to the predominantly Jewish owners of lending capital. Thus is the German farmer population torn up by the roots.

From John Bradshaw Holt, *German Agricultural Policy, 1918-1934 (Chapel Hill: The University of North Carolina Press, 1936), pp. 182-183, 185-187.*

THE AGRARIAN PROGRAM OF THE NATIONAL SOCIALIST
GERMAN LABOR PARTY (N.S.D.A.P.) OF MARCH, 1930:

(1) German soil, taken and defended by the German people
provides a living area and the means of subsistence for the whole
people.

(2) Only German folk comrades may be in possession of German
soil.

(3) Land possession acquired lawfully by German folk comrades
is regarded as inheritable property. To this property right, however,
is attached the duty to use the soil for the good of the whole people.
Vigilance regarding this obligation is the task of vocational courts,
which are composed of representatives of vocational divisions of
the agricultural population.

(4) German soil must not be an object of financial speculation and
must not be the source of effortless income of the owner. In the
future only a person can acquire land who cultivates it himself.
Therefore the state has preemption rights at every sale of land and
soil. The use of land and soil to secure debts to private money
lenders is prohibited.

(5) For the use of German soil the owner must pay to the state a
tax in keeping with the quality of the property. Beyond this land rent
tax any further state taxation of agricultural land and farms is not
permissible.

(6) Concerning the size of farms no systematic regulation is
possible.

(7) Inheritance rights to land and soil are to be so adjusted by
means of entail that a parceling and a burdening of the farms with
indebtedness will be avoided.

(8) The state reserves the right of expropriation with reasonable
indemnification (a) of land not in possession of a German folk
comrade, (b) of land which, according to the appropriate vocational
courts, has been farmed so irresponsibly as no longer to serve in
supplying food to the German people, (c) of portions of land
property not farmed by the owner himself to be used for the
settlement on the land of freehold farm homesteads, (d) of land
needed for special state uses (transportation and defense) for the
sake of the people as a whole. Land acquired unlawfully (in the
German sense) will be expropriated without remuneration.

(9) The state assumes the task of carrying out a land settlement

program with the acquired land in keeping with the standpoint of an important population policy. The land shall be lent to the settlers with inheritance rights at first under conditions which make possible continued and productive farming. The choice of settlers will be determined by an investigation of their civic and vocational fitness as settlers. Farmers' sons not enjoying inheritance rights will be especially considered. Above all is the land settlement along the eastern border important. But this task is not alone to be accomplished by the creation of farm homesteads, rather only in connection with the development of towns with strong buying power in agricultural areas together with a new distribution of branches of industry. In this way only will the marketing opportunities be created which will make existence possible for the new homestead farms.

The acquisiton of food supply and colonization areas for the growing German people is the task of the German foreign policy.The state has the task of furthering the economic cultural level of the farm population to correspond to its importance for the whole German people and to remove in this way one of the chief causes of the flight from the farms.

THE IMMEDIATE PROGRAM

(1) First of all, the present pressing needs of the country population must be remedied by tax adjustments and other particular measures. A halt must be called to the increasing indebtedness of agriculture by a legislated reduction of the interest rate for lending capital to the prewar level and by a severe action against usury.

(2) The state must see to it in its economic policy that agricultural work pays. Domestic production must be protected by import duties, government regulation of imports, and a consciously planned national education. The price formation for agricultural products must be withdrawn from the speculative influences of the produce exchanges, and the exploitation of farmers by wholesale distributors must be made impossible. The taking over of the cooperatives is to be encouraged by the state.

The vocational organizations have the task of reducing the production costs of agriculture and of increasing production.

(3) The vocational organizations have also the duty of building the farm labor vocational groups into the farm vocational com-

munity by means of socially fair and just labor contracts. The state assumes the right to supervise and arbitrate. An opportunity must be given to farm laborers to rise to the position of farm settlers. The necessary improvement of living conditions and wages for the farm laborers will improve the quicker and the more extensively the more the conditions of agriculture as a whole improve. By the virtue of these improvements in the condition of the native farm laborer and by the reduction of the flight from the land, the use of foreign labor will become unnecessary and therefore forbidden in the future.

(4) The importance of the farm population for the German people requires state and vocational advancement of vocational education and the revival of farm cultural life (farm youth homes, farm secondary schools, and the providing of extensive advantages for talented farm youth with no means).

KURT G. W. LUDECKE
The Appeal to Fear

The two selections which follow are included as literate examples of explanation and justification for upper middle class support of the Nazis. Both Kurt Ludecke and Ernst Hanfstaengl believed that the values of Imperial Germany were being destroyed by the Weimar Republic, and that Hitler would restore them. In this they were typical of many members of the middle-class elite who looked back to their former days of power shared with the Junker class and the military.

To UNDERSTAND the defunct German Republic and the amazing story of the Nazi triumph, one must realize that the "revolution" of Novmember 1918 had been no true revolution but a general breakdown and compromise on the part of all factions. When the military commanders at home surrendered to the street in the most cowardly capitulation of all time, and the generals in the field accepted the revolutionary *coup* as an accomplished fact, the "new" men in Berlin who had lived in fear of the strength and

Reprinted with the permission of Charles Scribner's Sons from *I Knew Hitler*, pages 2-14, by Kurt G.W. Ludecke. Copyright 1937 Kurt G.W. Ludecke; renewal copyright © 1965.

loyalty of the army were astounded to find that the power was theirs; that it had, in fact, virtually been forced upon them at a time when the state machine was at dead-center.

But the burden of power weighed heavily; the new "leaders" were actually afraid of it, for they did not know how to govern. Largely under the guidance of intellectual Jews, they were by no means genuine Red revolutionists, but petty bourgeois backed by workers of bourgeois sympathies. . . . Being without talent for government, without ideas or ideals, instead of fighting relentlessly for the realization of their Marxian theories, they did everything that might tend to encourage their enemies. Soon those irreconcilable enemies, Communists and Tories, discovered that they had little to fear, and much to gain by unscrupulous activity.

Thus the new regime found itself confronted on one hand by the "Red Menace" and the other by internal intrigues set afoot by the old military order, which had adroitly saddled the governmental authorities with the responsibility for the armistice and the shackles of the Versailles Treaty. The Republic was soon the plaything of the moneyed interests, a tool for speculation, greed, and unsocial aims. Old groups of influence and power, who under the Empire had screened their ambitions by standing behind the militarized nobles, the Junkers, and the nominal masters of industry, now stepped brazenly into the open in partnership with Jews who even before the war had controlled vital national interests. Old parties took new names and appeared in the political arena with the same men. The press was conscienceless, printing what it pleased without regard for either the truth or the national welfare. The war-bred apathy of the people permitted scandals to continue. And the one real and concrete power, the mighty old German army, which under able guidance could have set this madhouse in order, had disappeared as one of the penalties of the surrender to the Allies. . . .

The collapse of the poorly organized Nationalist revolt known as the Kapp-Putsch and the liquidation of the Communist rebellions gave Marxian Berlin a breathing-spell, however, and enabled it to set about the liquidation of the old nationalist Germany, and to attempt its moral and material disarmament. The way now seemed open for foes inside and outside the country to exterminate the remaining groups of national activists.

National circles could no longer postpone a showdown with the forces working to destroy the state, and in this critical hour the national movement of "Voelkische" or "folkic" resistance was born.

. . . The Kapp-Putsch, though a failure, had nevertheless brought to Bavaria a government of the Right, headed by Doctor Gustav von Kahr. . . . Munich thus became the stronghold of patriotic resistance dedicated to national rebirth, the stamping-ground of violent anti-republicans and anti-Jews, many of them Prussian political activists now being sought by the Berlin police. . . . The immediate problem was that of their own existence: the necessity of retaining and increasing their followers. The result was an intensified rivalry among themselves which made the cleavage between the merely nationalist and the folkic or racialist elements more apparent.

No master-leader rose up to unite these conflicting organizations in their one common aim—the fight against Berlin. Yet there was not room enough in Germany for them all to exist. The struggle for the survival of the fittest began to run its course through jealousies and conspiracies, in which antagonisms alternated with alliances as expediency might demand. Violence increased everywhere, fear and uncertainty were in the air, and the huge, helpless body of the German people drifted along in aimless, planless fashion, with little hope for the future.   This was the situation in Germany when I set about looking for a leader and a cause.

There was a hard apprenticeship ahead of me. I made the rounds, going from place to place, from group to group, confused, bewildered, diving now and again into the mad scramble for diversion that surrounded me, but unhappy always with a nostalgia for the proud Germany of my youth. I was looking for the German soul, or rather for the leader who would know how to reanimate it, and I was resolved not to desert again. . . .

I found [guidance] in Berlin in the person of Count Ernst zu Reventlow, well-known editor of the *Reichswart,* a folkic and uncompromisingly anti-Jewish weekly. . . . Long talks with the Count, in Berlin and at his home in Potsdam, helped me. I was frank about myself, and he understood the problems that vexed me, having already solved some of them for himself. Accepted and guided by such a man, whose word counted for much in folkic circles, I felt less lost.

This was in the first days of July, [1922], and troubled days they were. In June the O.C. had shocked the world with their assassination of Walther Rathenau, the Jewish minister of foreign affairs, not long after their killings of Reichsminister Mathias Erzberger, despised signer of the Armistice. Within a week the Mark fell from three hundred to twelve hundred to the dollar. Germany groaned; desperate rumors were whispered about. . . .

. . . Reventlow suggested that I go with him to Munich, where the political situation was taking on even deeper color. He had said that he would introduce me to General Ludendorff, and now he began to talk also of Dr. Pittinger and of one Adolf Hitler.

. . . Munich was still the city of charm, but with each visit I found its political aspect more absorbing. The constrast with Berlin was marked; one was the Mecca of Marxists and Jews, the other the citadel of their enemies.

. . . The drastic new laws were threatening the sovereignty of Bavaria, and relations between Berlin and Munich were strained. . . . The wave of indignation that surged through the land reached its climax in a huge mass demonstration of protest in Munich on August 11, 1922, under the sponsorship of the "Vaeterlandische Verbaende," which was, in effect, a holding company loosely coordinating all the patriotic societies, large and small, and including at that time the Nazi Party—the National Socialist German Workers' Party.

This was the greatest mass demonstration Munich had ever seen. It was one of incalculable historical importance, for on that day a little-known figure stepped into the light as a recognized public speaker of extraordinary power. This was a man who until then had been snubbed by the higher-ups in the patriotic societies. Now, because of his growing local importance and for the sake of a united front, he had been invited to appear as one of two speakers on a program in which all were taking part.

Adolf Hitler was scheduled to speak last.

It needed no clairvoyance to see that here was a man who knew how to seize his opportunity. Red placards announced in huge black letters that he was to appear. Many who read them had never even heard his name. Here was inflammatory slogans: "Versailles: Germany's Ruin . . . Republic of the People or State of the Jews? . . . International Solidarity: A Jewish World Swindle . . . Down with the November Criminals . . . The National Socialist Movement Must Conquer. . . . "

And every one of his placards ended with the blunt phrase: "Jews Not Admitted."

It was a bright summer day. . . . The "Patriotic Societies" had assembled without bands and without flags. But when the Nazis marched into the Koenigsplatz with banners flying, their bands playing stirring German marches, they were greeted with tremendous cheers. An excited, expectant crowd was now filling the beautiful square to the last inch and overflowing into surrounding streets. There were well over a hundred thousand. . . .

Reventlow had seen to it that we were near the speakers' stand. I was close enough to see Hitler's face, watch every change in his expression, hear every word he said.

When the man stepped forward on the platform, there was almost no applause. He stood silent for a moment. Then he began to speak, quietly and ingratiatingly at first. Before long his voice had risen to a hoarse shriek that gave an extraordinary effect of an intensity of feeling. There were many high-pitched, rasping notes—Reventlow had told me that his throat had been affected by war-gas—but despite its strident tone, his diction had a distinctly Austrian turn, softer and pleasanter than the German.

Critically I studied this slight, pale man, his dark hair parted on one side and falling again and again over his sweating brow. Threatening and beseeching, with small, pleading hands and flaming, steel-blue eyes, he had the look of a fanatic.

Presently my critical faculty was swept away. Leaning from the tribune as if he were trying to impel his inner self into the consciousness of all these thousands, he was holding the masses, and me with them, under a hypnotic spell by the sheer force of his conviction.

He urged the revival of German honor and manhood with a blast of words that seemed to cleanse. "Bavaria is now the most German land in Germany!" he shouted, to roaring applause. Then, plunging into sarcasm, he indicted the leaders in Berlin as "November Criminals," daring to put into words thoughts that Germans were now almost afraid to think and certainly to voice.

It was clear that Hitler was feeling the exaltation of the emotional response now surging up toward him from his thousands of hearers. His voice rising to passionate climaxes, he finished his speech with an anthem of hate rising against the "Novemberlings" and a pledge of undying love for the Fatherland. "Germany must be free!" was his final defiant slogan. Then two last words that were like the sting of a lash:

"Deutschland Erwache!"

Awake, Germany! There was thunderous applause. Then the masses took a solemn oath "to save Germany in Bavaria from Bolshevism."

I do not know how to describe the emotions that swept over me as I heard this man. His words were like a scourge. When he spoke of the disgrace of Germany, I felt ready to spring on any enemy. His appeal to German manhood was like a call to arms, the gospel he preached a sacred truth. He seemed another Luther. I forgot everything but the man; then, glancing around, I saw that his magnetism was holding these thousands as one.

Of course I was ripe for this experience. I was a man of thirty-two, weary of disgust and disillusionment, a wanderer seeking a cause; a patriot without a channel for his patriotism, a yearner after the heroic without a hero. The intense will of the man, the passion of his sincerity seemed to flow from him into me. I experienced an exaltation that could be likened only to religious conversion.

I felt sure that no one who had heard Hitler that afternoon could doubt that he was the man of destiny, the vitalizing force in the future of Germany. The masses who had streamed into the Koenigs-platz with a stern sense of national humiliation seemed to be going forth renewed.

The band struck up, the thousands began to move away. I knew my search was ended. I had found myself, my leader, and my cause.

ERNST HANFSTAENGL
The Appeal to Power

TIME AND AGAIN I [Hanfstaengl] noticed that during the first part of his [Hitler] speeches he stood with his knees braced back, rigid and immobile, until he provided the first sounding shot which brought a response. Every speech he gave had a past, a present and a future. Each appeared to be a complete historical survey of the situation and although his gift of phrase and argument was infinite in its variety, one sentence always reoccurred at an early stage: 'When we ask ourselves today what is happening in the world, we are obliged to cast our minds back to. . . . ' That was the sign that he had his audience under control and, taking the events leading up to the

From Ernst Hanfstaengl, *Hitler, The Missing Years,* ed. by Brian Connell (London: Eyre and Spottiswoode, 1957), pp. 68-69.

collapse of the Kaiser's Germany, he would build up the whole pyramid of the current situation according to his own lights.

The gestures which had so impressed me the first evening I saw him were as varied and flexible as his arguments. They were not, as in other speakers, stereotyped movements to find some employment for his hands, but an integral part of his method of exposition. The most striking, in contrast to the dull slamming of the fist into the palm of the other hand of so many orators, was a soaring upward movement of the arm, which seemed to leave infinite possibilities piercing the air. It had something of the quality of a really great orchestral conductor who instead of just hammering out the downward beat, suggests the existence of hidden rhythms and meaning with the upward flick of his baton.

To continue the musical metaphor, the first two-thirds of Hitler's speeches were in march time, growing increasingly quicker and leading up to the last third which was primarily rhapsodic. Knowing that a continuous presentation by one speaker would be boring, he would impersonate in a masterful way an imaginary opponent, often interrupting himself with a counter-argument and then returning to his original line of thought after completely annihilating his supposed adversary. There was a curious tinge to the finale. It was gradually being borne in on me that Hitler was a narcissus type for whom the crowd represented a substitute medium for the woman he did not seem able to find. Speaking for him represented the satisfaction of some depletion urge, and to me this made the phenomenon of his oratory more intelligible. The last eight to ten minutes of a speech resembled an orgasm of words.

I hope it will not appear too blasphemous when I say that he had learnt a lot from the Bible. He was to all intents and purposes an atheist by the time I got to know him, although he still paid lipservice to religious beliefs and certainly acknowledged them as the basis for the thinking of others. His pattern of looking into the past and then repeating the basis of his beliefs four times over derived directly from the New Testament, and no one can say it was not a proven method. His political arguments were based on what I came to call the system of the horizontal figure of eight. He would move out to the right, expend his criticism and curve round to the left for approval. He would continue on to reverse the process and come back dead centre to end up with *Deutschland über alles* to a roar of joint applause. He would attack the former ruling classes for their surrender of the nation, their class prejudices and feudal economic system to applause from the Left-Wingers, and then riddle those who were prepared to decry the true traditions of German greatness to the applause of the Right-Wingers. By the time he had finished he had everyone agreeing with everything that he had said. It was an art no one else in Germany possessed and my absolute conviction that it must in due course lead him to the top of the political pile only confirmed my intention of staying as near to him as I could.

WERNER VON BLOMBERG
The Party and the Military

Hitler could not have come to power without the support of the military. The following selection from War Minister Werner von Blomberg removes any shred of doubt that the brass of the German military accepted Hitler.

HITLER EMPHASIZED the "Soldatentum," the selection of capable men, and the re-establishment of German sovereignty within the German frontiers. These were aims to which any healthy nation would give its approval after a defeat, as France had done with great success after 1870-71. . . . In the early years of his regime Hitler stressed his adherence to the historical tradition of which the "Tag von Potsdam" represented and continued to represent for the German people a confession of faith. During these years we soldiers had no cause to complain of Hitler. He fulfilled hopes which were dear to all of us. If the generals no longer choose to remember this, it is obviously a case of deliberate forgetfulness. No thinking soldier could shut his eyes to the fact that after 1933 rearmament commensurate with the greatness of Germany could only be carried out with Hitler's help. . . . The German people agreed with the Hitler of those days. The masses obtained tangible advantages in the matter of social justice, the labor market, and above all an increasing importance of Germany as a political body. How could we soldiers, who had continually to deal with the masses, think otherwise! Whoever asserts the contrary now is betrayed by

From Telford Taylor, *Sword and Swastika: Generals and Nazis in the Third Reich* (New York: Simon and Schuster, 1952), pp. 113-115.

his memory. Moreover the Hitler regime was internationally organized. How otherwise could the Pilsudski agreement and the naval treaty have been achieved? During my sojourn in London in May, 1937, as "Coronation Delegate," I was able to ascertain everywhere indications of an improvement in the international situation vis-a-vis Germany. Until Hitler entered upon the period of aggressive politics, whether one dates it from 1938 to 1939, the German people had no decisive reason for hostility to Hitler, we soldiers least of all. He had not only given us back a position of respect in the life of the German people, and had freed all Germans from what we considered to be the shame of the Treaty of Versailles, but by the rearmament of Germany, which only Hitler could achieve, he had given the soldiers a larger sphere of influence, promotion and increased respect.

No general raised any objection then, or offered any resistance. That would have appeared absurd to us all then, even to those who now think otherwise. The approval of the younger officers may well have been more lively and more convincing than that of the older ones, but what now appears in retrospect, to some generals, as a refusal to accept Hitler was, I am convinced, merely the traditional resistance to anything new.

. . . Not one of them retired or refused promotion because Hitler was at the helm. I have observed, many many times, how our officers behaved personally vis-a-vis Hitler.

Up until 1938 there was no sign of hostility. . . . We soldiers had no reason to complain. Whoever speaks now of his opposition to Hitler in the years up to 1938-1939 has been betrayed by his memory. . . .

. . . To sum up I would say that Hitler in the first period which lasted at least up to 1938 strove to obtain the trust of us soldiers, with complete success. . . .

. . . One should not repudiate that to which one formerly gave approval in the main. Hitler proved fatal for the German people, but there were years, at first, when we believed that in a positive sense he was Germany's man of destiny.

HENRY ASHBY TURNER, JR.
The Party and Big Business

The old argument that a conspiracy between the Army and Big Business brought Hitler to power will not withstand careful research. Every segment of German society contributed a share of the support necessary to his expensive campaigns.contrary to the earlier literature on the subject, Big Business not only did not finance Hitler's rise to power, but it also did not give him appreciable moral support in the crucial years before 1933. One could, in fact, make a better case for support, both monetary and moral, from small and middle-sized business.

DID GERMAN big business support Adolf Hitler's climb to power? A quarter of a century after the demise of the Third *Reich,* this remains one of the major unresolved questions about its inception. For Marxists, or at least those who adhere to the Moscow line, the answer to this question has never been a problem. From the outset, they have viewed Nazism as a manifestation of "monopoly capitalism" and the Nazis as tools of big business.[1] Among non-

[1]According to the thesis that was long accepted in Communist circles, National Socialism was built up and installed in power by a conspiracy of the "monopoly capitalists" (viewed as a virtually monolithic group) and the reactionary *Junker,* whose aim was to suppress the working class and to launch an imperialist war. (See, e.g., Albert Norden, *Lehren deutscher Geschichte: Zur politischen Rolle des Finanz-kapitals und der Junker* [East Berlin, 1947].) Recently, more complex and differen-tiated interpretations have begun to appear, apparently as a result of the relaxation of ideological controls following Stalin's death. These studies view the rise of Hitler as the product of "contradictions" within the capitalist system that pit rival groups of "monopoly capitalists" against each other in a struggle for power. According to these interpretations, which are not heavily dependent upon evidence and thus vary considerably in particulars, the political events that brought Hitler to office were mere surface expressions of behind-the-scenes power struggles in the less visible, but nevertheless decisive, economic sphere. (See, e.g., Isakhar M. Faingar, *Die Entwick-lung des deutschen Monopolkapitals* [East Berlin, 1959], a translation of a Soviet book first published in 1958; Eberhard Czichon, *Wer verhalf Hitler zur Macht? Zum Anteil der deutschen Industrie an der Zerstörung der Weimarer Republik* [Cologne, 1967], a book by an East German writer; Kurt Gossweiler, "Die Rolle des monopolkapitals bei der Herbeiführung der Röhm-Affäre," doctoral dissertation, Humboldt University, 1963.)

From Henry Ashby Turner, Jr., "Big Business and the Rise of Hitler," *American Historical Review,* LXXV (October, 1969), 56-70. Reprinted by permission of Henry Ashby Turner, Jr.

Marxists there has been no such unanimity. Some have in large measure agreed with the Marxist interpretation;[2] others have rejected it.[3] Most have adopted a cautious middle position, asserting that some capitalists aided the Nazis but avoiding any precise analysis of the extent or effectiveness of that aid.[4] This wide range of views is in part clearly the product of ideological differences. But another factor has been the scanty, sometimes ambiguous, and frequently dubious nature of the evidence on which all previous studies of the subject rest. Few aspects of the history of National Socialism have, in fact, been so inadequately researched. Now that new documentation is available, the time has come for another look at the problem.

None of the new evidence contradicts the widespread impression that German big businessmen were unenthusiastic about the Weimar Republic. Most were not, as is often assumed, unreconstructed monarchists; they displayed, on the whole, a surprising indifference to governmental forms. What offended them about the new state was its adoption of costly welfare measures, its introduction of compulsory arbitration in disputes between labor and management, and, most particularly, the influence it accorded to the prolabor Social Democratic party, which was most pronounced in the government of the largest federal state, Prussia. Despite abundant objective evidence that the republic, at least during its years of prosperity, provided generally favorable conditions for business enterprise, Germany's business leaders continued to eye it with misgiving. Their attitude had much in common with that of the army: they, too,

[2]See George W.F. Hallgarten, *Hitler, Reichswehr und Industrie: Zur Geschichte der Jahre 1918-1933* (Frankfurt a.M., 1955); Arthur Schweitzer, *Big Business in the Third Reich* (Bloomington, Ind., 1964); Franz Neumann, *Behemoth: The Structure and Practice of National Socialism* (New York, 1942), the work of an independent scholar of Marxist background.

[3]Some examples are August Heinrichsbauer, *Schwerindustrie und Politik* (Essen, 1948); Seymour Martin Lipset, *Political Man: The Social Bases of Politics* (New York, 1960); Louis P. Lochner, *Tycoons and Tyrants: German Industry from Hitler to Adenauer* (Chicago, 1954); Edward N. Peterson, *Hjalmar Schacht: For and against Hitler* (Boston, 1954).

[4]See Alan Bullock, *Hitler: A Study in Tyranny* (London, 1952); Karl Dietrich Bracher, *Die Auflösung der Weimarer Republik: Eine Studie zum Problem des Machtverfalls in der Demokratie* (2d ed., Stuttgart, 1957); S. William Halperin, *Germany Tried Democracy: A Political History of the Reich from 1918 to 1933* (New York, 1946); Helmut Heiber, *Die Republik von Weimar* (Munich, 1966); and William L. Shirer, *The Rise and Fall of the Third Reich: A History of Nazi Germany* (New York, 1959).

refused to commit themselves to the new state, regarding it as a potentially transitory phenomenon, while viewing themselves as the guardians of something of more permanent value to the nation—in their case, *die Wirtschaft,* the industrial sector of the economy.[5]

In spite of its reserved attitude toward the new German state, big business was nevertheless politicized by the changes resulting from the Revolution of 1918. Whereas in the Empire its leaders had been able to influence governmental policy without wholesale commitment to partisan politics, in the republic they found it necessary to assume a more active political role.[6] In far greater numbers than in the Empire, they joined the ranks of the *bürgerlich,* or non-socialist, parties and sought places in the Parliaments for themselves or their spokesmen.[7] For most big businessmen, politics was more a matter of interests than of ideology.[8] When they took the trouble to describe their political outlook, the words that reoccurred with greatest frequency were "national" and "liberal." The term "liberal" has always been problematical in German usage, but in business circles of this period it was more so than usual, as was revealed by one businessman who, writing to an acquaintance, explained: "As you well know, I have always been liberal, in the sense of Kant and Frederick the Great."[9]

Although big business entered the politics of the republic, it never

[5]This theme runs through the speeches of big businessmen during the entire republican period. Many of these can be found in the *Veröffentlichungen* of the national association of industry, the *Reichsverband der Deutschen Industrie* (Berlin, 1919-32).

[6]Two recent studies of the political role of big business in the Empire are Lamar Cecil, *Albert Ballin: Business and Politics in Imperial Germany, 1888-1918* (Princeton, N.J., 1967); and Hans Jaeger, *Unternehmer in der deutschen Politik (1890-1918)* (Bonn, 1967).

[7]See Ingolf Liesebach, "Der Wandel der politischen Führungsschicht der deutschen Industrie von 1918 bis 1945," doctoral dissertation, University of Basel, 1957.

[8]On February 18, 1919, Albert Vögler, a prominent figure in the steel industry who had been elected to the National Assembly as a delegate of the German People's party, caused considerable consternation among his fellow deputies by announcing in his maiden speech to the chamber: "I speak here as the representative of an industry. . . . " *(Verhandlungen der verfassunggebenden deutschen Nationalversammlung, CCCXXVI, 137.)* Thereafter, the parliamentary spokesmen of big business tended to be more discreet in their public statements.

[9]Karl Zell, member of the *Vorstand of Kronprinz A.G. für Metallindustrie,* to Witkugel, Apr. 27, 1933, Papers of the Geman People's party *(Deutsche Volkspartei),* No. 151, *Deutsches Zentralarchiv,* Potsdam.

found a political home there. From the beginning, its spokesmen were scattered among the four principal nonsocialist parties, the Democratic party, the Catholic Center party, the German People's party, and the German National People's party. This dispersal divided and thus weakened the business leaders politically. Within each party they had to compete with numerous other pressure groups whose interests rarely coincided with their own and who could usually deliver far more votes. Sometimes the spokesmen of big business succeeded in gaining the backing of their parties, but more often they were defeated or forced to settle for less than they regarded as acceptable.[10] Contrary to the belief of the Marxists, economic power did not translate readily into political power in the Weimar Republic. And nowhere was this recognized more acutely than in big business circles.

The political impotence of money was strikingly demonstrated by the fate of a project that enjoyed wide support from big business during the last years of the republic. Having grown impatient with the multiplicity of parties with which they had to deal, a number of influential businessmen proposed the formation of a single, united nonsocialist party, a *bürgerliche Einheitspartei,* as it was generally labeled.[11] The plan called for such an organization to absorb the squabbling older parties, sweep away their superfluous and anachronistic ideological differences, and erect an impregnable barrier to Marxism. It was confidently expected, moreover, that in such a united party the interests of *die Wirtschaft* would at last receive their due. Much enthusiasm developed for this plan in the ranks of big business during the period 1930-1932. But although

---

[10] A striking example of this was the adoption in 1927 of national laws regulating the length of the industrial workday and establishing an unemployment insurance program despite the opposition of big business and despite the fact that the nonsocialist parties commanded a clear majority in the *Reichstag* and controlled the cabinet.

[11] There is much material on the project in the Paul Reusch Papers, *Historisches Archiv, Gute Hoffnungshütte,* Oberhausen; he was one of the most politically active of the Ruhr industrialists. Another source of information is the Fritz Klein Papers, which are in the possession of Klein's son, an East German historian who kindly made them available to me. Klein was the editor of the Berlin newspaper *Deutsche Allgemeine Zeitung* during the last years of the republic, when it was controlled by a consortium of big businessmen. (See also Friedrich Glum, *Zwischen Wissenschaft, Wirtschaft und Politik: Erlebtes und Erdachtes in vier Reichem* [Bonn, 1964], 395-407.)

considerable pressure was exerted on the politicians, including the withholding of financial contributions during election campaigns, nothing came of the project. Despite a barrage of importunities, threats, and punitive measures, the existing parties tenaciously defended their independence and the politicians their party posts. Again, the limits to the political utility of economic power had been revealed. The result was further disillusionment in big business circles, not only with the parties but with the democratic, parliamentary system as a whole—a disillusionment that deepened as a succession of unstable cabinets struggled unsuccessfully to cope with the Great Depression.

Crucial to the subject of this inquiry is the question of whether the unmistakably mounting discontent of big business led it to support Hitler and his movement during the last phases of the republic. The answer is, on the whole, no. The qualification is necessary because, as is well known, certain big businessmen, such as Fritz Thyssen, heir to one of the great steel enterprises of the Ruhr, did give money to the Nazis. If, however, one examines the political record of big business, it quickly becomes evident that these pro-Nazis are conspicuous precisely because they were exceptions. The failure to recognize this basic fact has led to great exaggeration of their importance, as has the reliance on untrustworthy sources, such as *I Paid Hitler,* a book published over the name of Thyssen, but not actually written by him.[12]

A number of legends about industrial support for the Nazis have been perpetuated by previous literature and, largely by virtue of repetition, have come to be accepted as fact. According to one of

---

[12]The book was prepared by a ghost writer, Emery Reves, on the basis of interviews with Thyssen in France during the spring of 1940, after the latter had fled Germany and denounced Hitler. Some of the draft chapters (in French) were seen and approved by Thyssen, but work on the book was interrupted by the breakthrough of the German armies on the western front in June 1940. Thyssen remained in France and was turned over to the Nazis by the Vichy regime for return to Germany, where he was imprisoned throughout the war. Reves escaped from France and finished the book, publishing it in English translation in New York and London in the autumn of 1941 [my citations will be to the New York edition]. Among the chapters not seen by Thyssen prior to publication were those treating his financial relations with the Nazis. My examination of the stenographic records of the interviews with Thyssen and the original draft chapters (still in the possession of Reves) has established that the book contains numerous spurious and inaccurate statements, even in the chapters approved by Thyssen.

these legends, large sums of money flowed to the Nazis through the hands of Alfred Hugenberg, the reactionary press lord who became head of the Right-wing German National People's party in 1928.[13] This allegation probably derives from Hugenberg's role in the campaign against the Young plan in 1929. As one of the organizations supporting that campaign, the Nazi party did receive a share of the funds that Hugenberg helped to raise at the time.[14] There is not a trace of documentary evidence, however, that any of Hugenberg's resources were thereafter diverted to the Nazis.[15] Indeed, this seems highly unlikely: as the leader of a party that was itself beset by financial problems, Hugenberg had little motive to share any funds he received from big business, least of all with a party that was taking votes away from his own.[16] The amount of big business money at Hugenberg's disposal has, in any event, been grossly exaggerated. Contrary to the widespread belief that he was one of the foremost spokesmen of big business throughout the republican period, most of the industrial backers of his party had opposed his election as its chairman in 1928, rejecting him as too inflexible, too provocative, and too highhanded for their tastes.[17] In the summer of 1930 a large segment of his party's industrial wing took issue with his opposition to Heinrich Brüning's cabinet and seceded to join the

---

[13]This view was first widely circulated by the journalist Konrad Heiden in *Adolf Hitler: Das Zeitalter der Verantwortungslosigkeit* (2 vols., Zürich, 1936-37), I, 268-72. Since then it has been repeated in many other studies of Hitler's rise, including the most recent book by Karl Dietrich Bracher, *Die deutsche Diktatur: Entstehung, Struktur, Folgen des Nationalsozialismus* (Cologne, 1969), 176.

[14]There is documentation on the finances of the plebiscite against the Young plan in two collections in the *Deutsches Zentralarchiv*, Potsdam: *Alldeutscher Verband*, No. 501; Stahlhelm, No. 25.

[15]The only evidence ever cited to support the allegations about Hugenberg's aid to Hitler is a passage in Thyssen, *I Paid Hitler*, 102-103. But as Bullock has observed *(Hitler,* 157), that passage is unclear as to when the alleged financing of Hitler took place. Since the passage was not written by Thyssen or even seen by him prior to publication, there are, moreover, grounds for doubting its authenticity. (See note 12, above.)

[16]See the papers of the German National People's party, *Deutsches Zentralarchiv,* Potsdam; see also Reusch Papers; Klein Papers.

[17]There is evidence of this opposition in the papers of Hugenberg's predecessor as party chairman, Count Kuno von Westarp, now in the possession of his family in Gärtringen, West Germany; in the Reusch Papers; and in the files of the *Verein Deutscher Eisen- und Stahlindustrieller,* R 13 I/1064, 1065, *Bundesarchiv,* Koblenz; see also Manfred Dörr, "Die Deutschnationale Volkspartei 1925 bis 1928," doctoral dissertation, University of Marburg, 1964, 448, n. 131.

new Conservative People's party.[18] Even among those who did not take that step, there was a strong movement to replace Hugenberg with a more moderate man.[19] As a result, Hugenberg, who had enjoyed wide support from big business during the first decade of the republic, was forced, during its last years, to rely increasingly upon the backing of agricultural interests.[20]

Another persistent legend concerns Emil Kirdorf, long universally regarded as a kind of industrial *alter Kämpfer*.[21] Kirdorf, an octogenarian survivor of the beginning phase of German heavy industry in the 1870's, was the first really noteworthy business figure to join the Nazi party, entering in 1927. But despite the tributes lavished upon him by Hitler and the party press during the Third *Reich,* he was far from a loyal Nazi. In 1928, only a little over a year after joining the party, Kirdorf resigned in anger, a fact that the Nazis long succeeded in concealing from historians.[22] Eventually, it is true, he rejoined the party, but only in 1934, when on personal orders from Hitler Kirdorf's records were rewritten to make his membership seem uninterrupted. But during the crucial years 1929-1933 Kirdorf was a supporter of the German National

[18]On the revolt against Hugenberg in 1930, see the statement circulated in April by the organization of industrial representatives in the German National People's party, the text of which appears in the privately printed memoirs of Emil Kirdorf, *Erinnerungen, 1847-1930,* copy in the Emil Kirdorf Papers, now at the *Gelsenkirchener Bergwerks-A.G.,* Essen, 226-33.

[19]Especially active in this effort was Tilo von Wilmowsky, brother-in-law and close adviser of Gustav Krupp von Bohlen und Halbach as well as an influential figure in industrial circles in his own right. Among those considered as replacements for Hugenberg were Carl Goerdeler and Hjalmar Schacht. Documentation can be found in the Gustav Krupp von Bohlen und Halbach Papers, *Krupp-Archiv,* Villa Hügel, Essen; and in the Reusch Papers.

[20]By the time Hugenberg was appointed a minister by Hitler in 1933, with responsibility for both agricultural and economic affairs, he clearly functioned as a spokesman of the agricultural interests and thus as an opponent of industry, especially on the question of tariff policy which sharply divided the two at that time. (Dieter Petzina "Hauptprobleme der deutschen Wirtschaftspolitik 1932/33, " *Vierteljahrshefte für Zeitgeschichte, XV* [Jan. 1967], 45-55.)

[21]See Bracher, *Auflösung,* 292, 334; Bullock, *Hitler,* 133; Czichon, *Wer verhalf Hitler, passim;* Konrad Heiden, *Der Fuehrer* (Boston, 1944), 340-42, 356; Hallgarten, *Hitler, Reichswehr und Industrie, passim;* Hochner, *Tycoons and Tyrants,* 97-98; Neumann, *Behemoth,* 360; Gerhard Schulz, in K.D. Bracher *et al., Die nationalsozialistische Machtergreifung* (Cologne, 1960), 394.

[22]I have dealt in greater detail with this and other aspects of the case of Kirdorf in "Emil Kirdorf and the Nazi Party," *Central European History I (Dec. 1968), 324-44.*

People's party, not the Nazi party. Nor is there any evidence that Kirdorf contributed appreciable sums to the Nazis during the struggle for power. Since he had retired from all active business posts even before joining the party for the first time in 1927, he had no access to corporate or associational funds.[23] Anything he gave had to come from his own pocket, and he was not known as a man who spent his money either gladly or lavishly. Kirdorf's reputation as a patron of National Socialism rests not on documented facts but on a myth created in large measure by the Nazis themselves following his re-entry into the party, when they appropriated the aged industrialist as a symbol of respectability.

The reason for Kirdorf's resignation from the party is indicative of the attitude of most big businessmen toward National Socialism in the years before Hitler achieved power. Kirdorf did not withdraw because the Nazis were anti-democratic, aggressively chauvinistic, or anti-Semitic (even though he, like most business leaders, was himself not an anti-Semite). What drove him out of the party was the social and economic radicalism of the Left-wing Nazis. Like millions of other Germans of middle-class background, including big businessmen, Kirdorf was attracted to Nazism by its assertive nationalism and its implacable hostility toward Marxism, but like most big businessmen, he was at the same time repelled by the fear that the National Socialists might eventually live up to their name by turning out to be socialists of some kind. Hitler, who began earnestly to court the business community in 1926, went to great pains to allay this fear. In 1927, at the request of Kirdorf, he wrote a pamphlet that was secretly printed and then distributed in business circles by the old industrialist.[24] In the pamphlet, as in his speech before the Düsseldorf *Industrie-Klub* in January 1932, Hitler sought to indicate

[23]According to one legend still very much an article of faith in East German historical circles, Kirdorf in 1931 prevailed upon the bituminous coal cartel *(Rheinisch-Westfälisches Kohlensyndikat)* to impose a levy of five or in some versions fifty) pfennigs on each ton of coal sold, the proceeds to go to the Nazis (See Czichon, *Wer verhalf Hitler,* 19.) No documentary evidence has ever been introduced to support this allegation. It was challenged from a number of quarters when it first appeared in the postwar German press in 1947. (A collection of this material is located in the papers of the de-Nazification trial of Fritz Thyssen, *Hauptakte, 283-86, Hessisches Hauptstaatsarchiv,* Wiesbaden.) Overlooked by all who have repeated the allegation is the fact that Kirdorf's active role in the coal cartel had come to an end in April 1925. (Walter Bacmeister, *Emil Kirdorf Der Mann. Sein Werk* [2d ed., Essen (1936)], 100.)

[24]See Henry Ashby Turner, Jr., "Hitler's Secret Pamphlet for Industrialists,1927," *Journal of Modern History,* XL (Sept. 1968), 348-74.

that there was no need to fear socialism from his party. It is safe to assume that he said much the same thing in his numerous other meetings with representatives of big business.[25] His efforts, however, were repeatedly compromised, as in the case of Kirdorf, by the radical noises emanating from the Left Wing of the Nazi party.[26]

As a consequence, most of the political money of big business went, throughout the last years of the republic, to the conservative opponents of the Nazis.[27] In the presidential campaign of 1932 most

[25]Similar statements by Hitler appear in the recently discovered stenographic record of two conversations he had in the spring of 1931 with a business-oriented newspaper editor. (Edouard Calic, *Ohne Maske: Hitler-Breiting Geheimgespräche 1931* [Frankfurt a.M., 1968], 35-36.)

[26]Instances of this are too numerous to recount in full, but two more examples can be cited. In February 1926 Hitler delivered a lengthy speech before the Hamburg *Nationalklub von 1919*. (See Werner Jochmann, *Im Kampf um die Macht: Hitlers Rede vor dem Hamburger Nationalklub von 1919* [Frankfurt a.M., 1960].) Three years later a Nazi spokesman in Hamburg reported that the speech was still remembered favorably in business circles but that there was general alienation from the Nazi party as a consequence of the radical stance of the local leadership and the party's *Revolverpresse*. (Friedrich Bucher to Hitler, July 20, 1929, *Reichsleitung, Personalakte Hüttmann*, Berlin Document Center.) During the early part of 1932, Hitler sought to cultivate allies in big business circles, addressing industrial groups and instigating, through his adviser Wilhelm Keppler, the formation of an advisory group of businessmen, the later *Freundeskreis*. The effects were largely undone, however, by a campaign pamphlet for the summer *Reichstag* election, *Wirtschaftliches Sofortprogramm der N. S. D. A. P.* (Munich, 1932), which alarmed businessmen, by virtue of its anticapitalist slogans and its call for deficit spending and governmental controls aimed at ending unemployment. In September Hitler informed leading business circles through Schacht that distribution of the pamphlet had been stopped and that the remaining copies had been destroyed, but much damage had already been done by that time. (Schacht to Reusch, Sept. 12, 1932, No. 400101290/33, Reusch Papers.)

[27]In his conversation with the journalist Richard Breiting in May 1931, Hitler boasted that the Nazi party already enjoyed the financial backing of "Krupp, Schröder and others from big industry." (Calic, *Ohne Maske*, 27.) Only a few pages later, however, he told of his plans to win over big business, revealing that he regarded this as a task yet to be accomplished. (*Ibid.*, 28–29, 35, 37–38.) Further doubt is cast on the accuracy of Hitler's claim by the well-known coolness of Gustav Krupp von Bohlen und Halbach toward National Socialism prior to Hitler's appointment as Chancellor, an attitude recognized by authors of the most varied persuasions and confirmed by Krupp's private correspondence in the Krupp Papers. (See Czichon, *Wer verhalf Hitler*, 53; Hallgarten, *Hitler, Reichswehr und Industrie*, 117; Lochner, *Tycoons and Tyrant*, 139.) Baron Kurt von Schroeder (to whom the name "Schröder" apparently refers) may well have been aiding the Nazis by 1931, but he was an official of a medium-sized bank in a provincial city (Cologne), not a figure in "big industry" or even a confidant of the leading industrial circles. (See note 47, below.)

of the business community backed Paul von Hindenburg against Hitler, despite the Nazi leader's blatant appeal for support in his *Industrie-Klub* speech.[28] In the two *Reichstag* elections of 1932, big business was overwhelmingly behind the bloc of parties that supported the cabinet of Franz von Papen, the first government since the Revolution of 1918 to arouse enthusiasm in business circles.[29] If money could have purchased political power, the republic would have been succeeded by Papen's *Neuer Staat,* not by Hitler's *Drittes Reich.* But the effort to transform marks into votes proved a crushing failure.

There were, to be sure, exceptions to this pattern. Certain big businessmen did give money to the Nazis, particularly after the 1930 *Reichstag* election showed them to be a major political factor. Some of these contributions can best be described, however, as political insurance premiums. This was clearly the case, for example, with Friedrich Flick, a parvenu intruder into the ranks of the Ruhr industrialists, who by the early 1930's had managed to secure a dominant position in the country's largest steel-producing firm, the United Steel Works *(Vereinigte Stahlwerke).* Flick's speculative transactions and his questionable dealings with the Brüning cabinet left him vulnerable to attacks from the press and apprehensive about the attitude of future cabinets toward his enterprises.[30] His solution was to spread his political money across the political spectrum, from

[28]This is conceded even by Hallgarten. (*Hitler, Reichswehr und Industrie,* 106.) There is documentation on the fund-raising campaign in the papers of the industrialist who headed it, Carl Duisberg, cofounder of *I. G. Farben* and chairman of its board of overseers and its administrative council. (*Autographen-Sammlung von Dr. Carl Duisberg, Werksarchiv, Farbenfabrik Bayer,* Leverkusen.)

[29]There is abundant documentation to this effect in the Klein Papers, Krupp Papers, and Reusch Papers, as well as in the informative diary of Hans Schäffer, State Secretary in the Ministry of Finance, now located in the archive of the *Institut für Zeitgeschichte,* Munich. See also Hans Radandt, "'Freie Wahlen' und Monopolkapital," *Zeitschrift für Geschichtswissenschaft,* IX (No. 6, 1961), 1321–22. This East German publication provides details about a fund-raising meeting of industrialists in October 1932, but neglects to mention the use for which the funds were intended, thus leaving the impression they might have been destined for the Nazis. A report on the same meeting in the Reusch Papers makes clear, however, that the money raised would go to the Papen bloc, not to the Nazis. (Memo by Martin Blank, Oct. 19, 1932, No. 4001012024/10, Reusch Papers.)

[30]This emerged clearly from the testimony and documentary evidence in the Flick trial at Nuremberg in 1947. (See the published excerpts in Nuremberg Military Tribunals, *Trials of War Criminals before the Nuremberg Military Tribunal under Control Council Law No. 10* [15 vols., Washington, D.C., 1949-53], VI, *passim.* Flick was particularly vulnerable as a result of the purchase of his United Steel

the liberal and Catholic parties to the Nazi party. Flick may be a deplorable example of the politically amoral capitalist, but he was by no means an enthusiastic supporter of National Socialism prior to 1933. Nor is there any indication that he was especially generous toward the Nazis. According to the records he produced at his war crimes trial in Nuremberg, the Nazis received little more than token contributions in comparison to the sums that went to their opponents.[31]

The political activities of the *I. G. Farben* chemical trust were characterized by much of the same pattern as those of Flick. From its formation in 1925, the company maintained contact with all the nonsocialist parties and made financial contributions to them. According to the postwar accounts of one official of the trust, the Nazis were added to the list in 1932. That same official estimated the total contributions for one of the *Reichstag* election campaigns of 1932 (it is not clear whether he was referring to the July or November elections) at approximately 200,000 to 300,000 marks. Of this, he reported no more than 10 to 15 per cent had gone to the Nazis.[32] *I. G. Farben,* like Flick, had special reason to be concerned about maintaining the good will of the political parties. In its case, this concern arose from heavy investments in elaborate processes designed to yield high-grade synthetic gasoline. Since the costs of production were initially high, the company could hope to break into the domestic market only if a protective tariff were imposed on oil imports. Such a tariff had been put into effect by the Brüning cabinet and maintained by the Papen regime, but in view of Germany's obviously chronic political instability, the tariff question remained a source of considerable anxiety to the leadership of the firm. When

---

Works stock by the *Reich* in May 1932 at a price far above the market value. Hallgarten has alleged, although with no supporting evidence, that this "Gelsenkirchen Deal" forged a link in the summer of 1932 between the steel industry and the Nazi party by virtue of the Nazis' having suppressed a projected parliamentary investigation of the transaction. (Hallgarten, *Hitler, Reichswehr und Industrie,* 113.) Hallgarten's allegation has, however, been effectively refuted by an East German scholar. (Gerhard Volkland, "Hintergründe und politischen Auswirkungen der Geselkirchen-Affäre im Jahre 1932," *Zeitschrift für Geschichtswissenschaft, XI* [No. 2, 1963], 312-13.)

[31]For a summary, see *Trials of War Criminals,* VI, 382-83. The full documentation can be found in Record Group 238 (World War II War Crimes Records), Case 5, Dokumentenbuch Flick I, National Archives [hereafter cited as NA].

[32] See the affidavits of Max Ilgner, Microcopy T-30l (Records of the Office of the U.S. Chief Counsel for War Crimes, Nuremberg, Military Tribunals, Relating to Nazi Industrialists), roll 13/NI-1293, *ibid.;* T-301/55/NI-7082, *ibid.*

attacks on *Farben* appeared in the Nazi press in 1932, concern developed about the attitude of what was by then the country's strongest political party. Two minor officials were, accordingly, sent to Munich in the autumn of 1932 to sound out Hitler on the project.[33] Much has been made of this episode by some writers, who have inferred that it produced a deal that brought *Farben* behind the National Socialist movement at a crucial time.[34] From all available evidence, however, the firm's representatives came away with only vague assurances from Hitler that he would halt the attacks in the party press.[35] The Nazis apparently received at most the small share of the relatively modest political funds described above, although even this may, in view of the ambiguity of the evidence, have been granted earlier, at the time of the summer election campaign, and thus quite independently of the Munich meeting with Hitler. There is, in any case, no evidence that the chemical combine wanted a Nazi triumph or threw its financial support decisively to National Socialism. All indications are, in fact, that the leaders of *Farben,* acutely aware of their firm's dependence on exports, were apprehensive at the prospect of a take-over of the government by a party that preached economic autarky.[36]

[33]See *Trials of War Criminals,* VII, 536-54. The two young emissaries were Heinrich Bütefisch, a technical expert, and Heinrich Gattineau, a public relations specialist who had studied with Professor Karl Haushofer at the University of Munich and was thus aquainted with Rudolf Hess, who arranged the meeting.

[34]Czichon, *Wer verhalf Hitler,* 50; Albert Norden, *Die Nation und wir: Ausgewählte Aufsätze und Reden 1933-1964* (2 vols., East Berlin, 1965), I, 322: Schweitzer, *Big Business, 102.*

[35]See *Trials of War Criminals,* VII, 536-54; see also the full testimony in Record Group 238, Case 6 (German transcript), XXIV, XXV, XXXIV, NA; interrogation of Bütefisch, 1947, T-301/71/NI-8637, *ibid.* The prosecution sought to establish a connection between the meeting of Bütefisch and Gattineau with Hitler and an agreement of the *Reich* government with *Farben,* consummated in December 1933, which provided price supports for the synthetic gasoline project. This interpretation was rejected by both Bütefisch and Gattineau. It was also refuted by affidavits from officials in the Ministry of Economics who had drawn up the agreement of 1933 and who denied that any political influence had been involved. (Dokumentenbuch Bütefisch 4, Record Group 238, Case 6, *ibid.*)

[36]At a meeting of *Farben's* "Working Committee" (*Arbeitsausschuss*) *on April 15, 1932,* the relationship between the firm's plans for agreements with foreign companies and the autarkist slogan, "Protection of the German Market" (*Schutz des deutschen Marktes),* was discussed. Director August von Knieriem emphasized that it was the company's policy to oppose both autarky and state controls of any kind,

As in the cases of Flick and *I. G. Farben,* most of the big business money that found its way to the Nazis was not given simply, or even primarily, with the aim of bringing them to power. Whereas Flick and *Farben* were seeking to buy political insurance against the eventuality of a Nazi capture of the government, others were attempting to alter the nature of the Nazi movement. This they hoped to accomplish by giving money to "sensible" or "moderate" Nazis, thereby strengthening that element and weakening the economically and socially radical tendencies that had always been the chief obstacles to cooperation between big business and National Socialism. There was, however, no agreement as to who the "sensible" Nazis were. Thyssen, one of the few who really wanted a Nazi triumph, was nevertheless concerned about radicalism in the party. He sought to counteract it by subsidizing the man he regarded as the bulwark of moderation, Hermann Göring, who used at least a considerable portion to Thyssen's money to indulge his taste for lavish living.[37] Hermann Bücher, head of the large electrical equipment concern, *Allgemeine Elektrizitäts-Gesellschaft,* tried to combat Nazi radicalism by giving financial aid to Joseph Goebbels' rival in Berlin, storm troop leader Walter Stennes, in his short-lived revolt.[38] Surprisingly, the directors of the principal organization of the coal industry, the *Bergbau-Verein,* saw their "moderate" Nazi in Gregor Strasser—usually classified as a leader of the Left Wing—and for a time channeled funds to him.[39] Still others gave money to Walther Funk, the former editor of a conservative financial newspaper, who bore at least the title of economic adviser to Hitler and who was regarded in some business

pointing out that Carl Bosch, one of the founders of the combine, had recently made a similar statement to the press. (Nachtrag I zu den Dokumentenbüchern Gattineau [excerpt from the stenographic record of the meeting], Record Group 238, Case 6, NA.)

[37]Thyssen, *I Paid Hitler,* 100. This statement in the book is confirmed by the stenographic record of the interviews with Thyssen on which the book was based. (See note 12, above.)

[38]This is revealed by Bücher's correspondence with Reusch in No. 400101290/5, Reusch Papers.

[39]See the book written by the intermediary between Strasser and the *Bergbau-Verein* (properly *Verein für die bergbaulichen Interessen),* Heinrichsbauer, *Schwerindustrie und Politik,* 39-52. Czichon (*Wer verhalf Hitler,* 54) cites the as yet unpublished memoirs of Günther Gereke to the effect that the industrialist Otto Wolff also subsidized Strasser in 1932 at the request of Wolff's friend, General Kurt von Schleicher, who hoped thereby to make Strasser more independent of Hitler.

quarters as a "liberal" Nazi and a potential moderating influence.[40] Not all attempts to alter the Nazis' economic and social attitudes involved financial contributions. Kirdorf, for example, maintained cordial personal relations with Hitler even after resigning from the party in 1928 and sought to exert influence on the *Führer* by making clear his objections to the Left-wing Nazis and to the radical planks in the party program.[41] Much the same attempt was made by the *Keppler-Kreis,* the group of businessmen assembled in the spring of 1932 at Hitler's request by one of his advisers, Wilhelm Keppler. Later, during the Third *Reich,* after this group was appropriated by Heinrich Himmler and transformed into his *Freundeskreis,* it became a source of enormous contributions for the SS.[42] But prior to the acquisition of power by the Nazis, it was merely an advisory body,seeking without success, to bring about a commitment of the party to conservative economic policies; it did not serve as a channel for business contributions.[43]

The question of whether the Nazis were aided appreciably by the

[40]At Nuremberg in 1948 Flick described Funk as a "liberal thinking man" and a "man of liberal outlook." (See Record Group 238, Case 10 [German transcript], XV, 5584, NA) According to testimony of his former assistant, Otto Steinbrinck, Flick was among those who aided Funk. (Case 5 [German transcript], XV, 4981, *ibid.)* Funk also received small subsidies from two young public relations agents of *I. G. Farben,* who acted independently of each other in providing funds for the maintenance of his Berlin office in 1932. (See affidavit of Ilgner, May 1, 1947, T-301/55/NI-7082, *ibid.)* Ilgner stated that he ceased payments when he discovered that Funk was also receiving money from Gattineau for the same purpose. According to Heinrichsbauer (*Schwerindustrie und Politik,* 42, 44), the *Bergbau-Verein* also subsidized Funk.

[41]Turner, "Kirdorf and the Nazi Party," 335-36.

[42]Klaus Drobisch, "Der Freundeskreis Himmler," *Zeitschrift für Geschichtswissenschaft,* VIII (no. 2, 1960), 304-28.

[43]One of the founding members of the *Keppler-Kreis,* Baron Kurt von Schroeder, was repeatedly questioned about this after the war. On each occasion he denied that the group had made any financial contributions to the Nazi cause prior to the party's acquisition of power. (See T-301/3/NI-246, NI-247, NA; also, Pre-Trial Interrogations, Schroeder, Aug. 18, 1947, Record Group 238, *ibid.)* In an affidavit of December 5, 1945, Schroeder stated that fund raising began only in 1935 or 1936 when Himmler took over the group. (Record Group 238, PS-3337, *ibid.)* This statement agrees with that of Steinbrinck, another early member, who dated the start of fund raising as 1935. (Pre-Trial Interrogations, Steinbrinck, Jan. 25, 1947, Record Group 238, *ibid.)* See also the documentation on the beginnings of the *Keppler-Kreis* in the privately printed memoirs of Emil Helfferich, one of the founding members, *Ein Leben* (4 vols., Hamburg and Jever, 1948-64), IV, 9-26.

big business money that did reach them from those who were seeking either to buy protection or to alter the nature of the party cannot at present be definitively answered; ignorance about Nazi finances is a major handicap that deserves far more attention than it has received. But it is known, from Goebbels' diary and other sources, that the Nazis were plagued by acute money problems until the very moment of Hitler's appointment as Chancellor.[44] It thus seems clear that the sums received were not sufficient to solve the party's financial problems. The significant point, in any case, is that the funds reaching the Nazis from big business were but a small fraction of those that went to their opponents and rivals. On balance, big business money went overwhelmingly against the Nazis.

In spite of all this, it is nevertheless true that most business leaders were favorably inclined toward the new cabinet installed on January 30, 1933, with Hitler as Chancellor. It has been alleged that this was only the expression of attitudes already discernible at least as early as November, when, following the poor showing of the Papen bloc at the polls, some businessmen had, at the instigation of the *Keppler-Kreis,* petitioned Hindenburg to appoint Hitler Chancellor. But the attitude of those who signed the petition was not typical of the outlook of big business in November 1932; nor did the list of signatories include any major business figures, aside from Thyssen, who had for some time made no secret of his support for the Nazis. Another signatory, Hjalmar Schacht, is often assigned to the ranks

---

[44]Some writers have contended that Goebbels' diary, *Vom Kaiserhof zur Reichskanzlei: Eine historische Darstellung in Tagebuchblättern* (Munich 1934), shows the finances of the Nazis to have improved markedly in January 1933, following the meeting of Hitler with Papen at the house of the banker Schroeder. Shirer *(Rise and Fall,* 179), for example, citing Goebbels' entry of January 16, writes: "he reported that the financial position of the party had 'fundamentally improved overnight.'" There is, however, no mention of finances in that entry; the overnight change in the Nazis' fortunes referred to by Goebbels was clearly the result of the party's successes the day before in the state elections of Lippe, not of capitalists' contributions. The same erroneous interpretation has been given to this diary entry by Bracher. *(Auflösung,* 694, n. 33.) Bracher cites as well a second entry, that of January 5, in which Goebbels remarked that the financial situation of the Berlin *Gau* had somewhat improved. *(Vom Kaiserhof,* 235.) It is hardly likely, however, that the Hitler-Papen meeting of January 4 could have, as Bracher infers, had such an immediate material effect on the treasury of the local Berlin organization only one day later. In any event, by January 6 Goebbels was again bemoaning the "bad financial situation of the organization." *(Ibid.,* 236.)

of big business, but as of 1932 he is more properly classified as a political adventurer.[45]

The change of outlook occurred for most businessmen in December 1932; its primary cause was Kurt von Schleicher. It is difficult to exaggerate their distrust and fear of the man who became Chancellor on December 3. They were hostile to him in part for his role in bringing down Papen, the one Chancellor they had admired and trusted. But even more important was Schleicher's apparent indifference to orthodox economic principles and traditional class alignments. Shortly after becoming Chancellor he caused the gravest apprehension in business circles by announcing that he was neither a capitalist nor a socialist. He also flirted openly with trade unions, raising the specter of an alliance of the military and the working class against the propertied elements of society. As a result, Germany's big businessmen feared that Schleicher might turn out to be a socialist in military garb.[46] It was more from a desire to be rid of

[45]Schacht, a banker by background, had been out of private business for nine years, first as a government official and then, after his resignation as president of the Reichsbank in 1930, in retirement on his country estate. East German historians have made much of the discovery in their archives of twenty signed copies of the petition which reached President's Hindenburg's office. (See Albert Schreiner, "Die Eingabe deutscher Finanzmagnaten, Monopolisten und Junker an Hindenburg für die Berufung Hitlers zum Reichskanzler [November, 1932]," Zeitschrift für Geschichtswissenschaft, IV [No. 2, 1956], 366-69; also, Czichon, Wer verhalf Hitler, 41-42.) A comparison of the list of those who signed the petition with the list of those considered as potential signers by the organizers of the project reveals, however, that the great majority apparently refused to sign. (See Record Group 238, PS-3901, NA; excerpt in International Military Tribunal, Trial of the Major War Criminals before the International Military Tribunal, Nuremberg, 14 November 1945-1 October 1946 [42 vols., Nuremberg, 1947-49], XXXIII, 531-33.) It is also perhaps revealing that East German historians have made no mention of another document in the same archival file, also dating from November 1932: an election appeal issued by the Deutscher Ausschuss 'Mit Hindenburg für Volk und Reich,' calling for support in the November Reichstag election of the parties backing Papen's cabinet (and thus for opposition to the Nazis). In contrast to the 20 signed copies of the petition, this appeal bears 339 signatures, including those of some of the many prominent businessmen who did not sign the petition. (Büro des Reichspräsidenten, No. 47, Deutsches Zentralarchiv, Potsdam.)

[46]There is ample evidence of this in a wide variety of sources. For examples, see the letter of the manager of the Deutscher Industrie-und Handelstag, Eduard Hamm, to Otto Most, Dec. 10, 1932, in which Hamm wrote of rumors to the effect that the cabinet would be revamped on a parliamentary basis in a "certain soldier-worker direction," R11/10, Bundesarchiv, Koblenz; speech of Krupp to the Hauptausschuss of the Reichsverband der Deutschen Industrie, Dec. 14, 1932, reported in a communication of the Reichsverband of the Dec. 15, No. 400101220/13, Reusch

him than from enthusiasm for what was to replace him that they applauded the events of January 1933. Contrary to what has often been asserted, big business played no part in the intrigues of that month. Much has been made of the role of Baron Kurt von Schroeder, the banker at whose home in Cologne Hitler and Papen met on January 4 to conspire against Schleicher. Schroeder was, however, not acting as an agent of big business. His importance lay in the fortuitous fact that he was acquainted with both Papen and Keppler, Hitler's adviser, and could thus serve as a convenient intermediary between two sides anxious to join forces.[47] Nor is there any evidence that the meeting at his house began a flow of business money to the Nazis, as has repeatedly been alleged.[48]

Papers; excerpts from the speech of the manager of the *Reichsverband,* Jakob Herle, Jan. 2, 1933, Herle to Reusch, Jan. 4, No. 400101220/14, *ibid.;* Reusch's letters to Hamm, Dec. 22, 31, 1932, No. 40010123/25, *ibid.;* Duisberg to Herle, Jan. 9, 1933, *Reichsverband der Deutschen Industrie, Allgemeiner Schriftwechsel mit der Geschäftsführung, Werksarchiv, Farbenfabrik Bayer,* Leverkusen; Hugo Stinnes to Klein, Jan. 18, 1933, Klein Papers. Some of the leading Ruhr industrialists had an additional reason for hostility toward Schleicher, for they suspected he had used to buy himself a newspaper (*Tägliche Rundschau,* Berlin) some of the money they had given him during the July election campaign in support of the parties backing Papen. (See Kurt von Schleicher Papers, HO8-42/22, *Bundesarchiv,* Koblenz; Reusch to Fritz Springorum, Oct. 12, 1932, No. 400101290/36, Reusch Papers.

[47]The nature of Schroeder's role emerges from the correspondence preceding the meeting. (T-301/3/NI-200-16, NA.) Schroeder's lack of standing in big business circles prior to 1933 is attested to by the almost complete absence of his name from the correspondence of major industrial figures cited elsewhere in this article. As is shown by a series of postwar interrogations, his industrial role began only during the Third *Reich,* largely as a result of his Nazi contacts. (NI-226-49, *ibid.)*

[48]Hallgarten (*Hitler, Reichswehr und Industrie,* 116) has alleged that immediately after the meeting a consortium of industrialists gave a million marks to the SS and paid the most pressing election debts of the Nazi party. As evidence, he cites an undocumented assertion by the journalist Konrad Heiden, plus a postwar affidavit by Schroeder. In the affidavit Schroeder mentioned payment of a million marks a year to the SS by the *Freundeskreis,* but stated that this began only in 1935 or 1936, specifying that no such payments to the Nazis were made prior to then by that group (this document, which Hallgarten cites by its exhibit number in the Flick trial, is better known as PS-3337; see note 43, above). Two further supporting references offered by Hallgarten lead to an English translation of an excerpt from the same affidavit by Schroeder and pages "1353 ff." of a volume containing only 1099 pages. Bracher has accepted Hallgarten's interpretation and offered as additional evidence a quotation from Thyssen, *I Paid Hitler,* which refers not, as Bracher indicates, to the effects of the Cologne meeting, but to the aftermath of Hitler's speech before the *Industrie-Klub* almost a year earlier. (Bracher, *Auflösung,* 694, *n. 33; see also not 44, above.)* If the Cologne meeting had opened the coffers of big business to the Nazis, there would hardly have been need for Hitler's appeal for funds to the leaders of industry on February 20, 1933. (See *Trials of War Criminals,* VII, 555-68.)

Money was, in any event, not what mattered in January 1933. What counted was influence with Hindenburg, and big business had little or none of that. From the President's *Junker* standpoint, even the most powerful bankers and industrialists were little better than shopkeepers.[49]

Most of the leaders of big business were, to the very end, under a basic misapprehension about the nature of the new cabinet taking shape in January 1933. Their information came mainly from Papen and his circle, and they were led to believe that what was coming was a revival of the Papen cabinet, with its base widened through the inclusion of the Nazis. Even when it was learned that Papen would be Vice-Chancellor under Hitler, big business continued to assume that he would be the real leader of the new government.[50] In the eyes of the business community, January 30, 1933, seemed at first to mark the fall of the hated Schleicher and the return of the trusted Papen, not the advent of a Nazi dictatorship.

By the time the leaders of big business were disabused of this illusion, they were ready to make their peace with Hitler. One factor in this turn of events was the ability of the new Chancellor, as the legally installed head of government, to appeal to their respect for constituted authority. But even more important, once he was in office Hitler demonstrated that he was, as he had always reassured them, not a socialist. He therefore had no difficulty in extracting

[49]In early October 1931 former Chancellor Wilhelm Cuno, head of the Hamburg-America shipping line, met secretly with President Hindenburg and suggested some of the country's most prominent big businessmen for inclusion in a projected economic council. It quickly became evident, Cuno told editor Klein of the *Deutsche Allgemeine Zeitung* later the same day, that Hindenburg had not recognized most of the names. (Diary entry, Oct. 5, 1931, Klein Papers.) The relative unimportance of money in the political constellation of January 1933 was recognized by Goebbels, who wrote in his diary on January 6: "In view of the satisfying progress of political developments, one hardly has the desire to bother any more about the bad financial situation of the organization. If we pull it off this time, then all that will not matter any longer." (Goebbels, *Vom Kaiserhof,* 236.)

[50]On January 26, 1933, in a letter to the chairman of the *Reichsverband der Deutschen Industrie,* Ludwig Kastl, managing director of that organization and usually well informed on political developments, reported that the talk in Berlin was of a Papen-Hitler-Schacht cabinet, with Papen as Chancellor. (Kastl to Krupp, Dokumentenbuch von Bülow I, Record Group 238, Case 10, NA.) As late as March, Reusch described the new government as "Herr von Papen's work of political unification" and promised further support of Papen. (Reusch to Kurt von Lersner, Mar. 4, 1933, No. 400101293/12, Reusch Papers.) The expectation of a new Papen cabinet was widespread in late January. (See Ewald von Kleist-Schmenzin, "Die letzte Möglichkeit: Zur Ernennung Hitlers zum Reichskanzler am 30. Januar 1933," *Politische Studien,* X [Feb. 1959], 91.)

large sums from big business, starting with the campaign for the *Reichstag* election of March 1933. These contributions unquestionably aided Hitler significantly. But they aided him in the consolidation of his power, not in its acquisition. He had achieved that without the support of most of big business, indeed in spite of its massive assistance to his opponents and rivals.

These observations are in no sense intended as an exoneration of German big business. Its political record in the period that ended with the establishment of the Third *Reich* is hardly praiseworthy. In numerous ways its leaders contributed indirectly to the rise of Nazism; through their failure to support the democratic republic; through their blind hostility to the Social Democrats and the labor unions; through their aid to reactionary forces, most conspicuously the Papen regime; and through the respectability they bestowed upon Hitler by receiving him into their midst on a number of occasions. Some contributed more directly, by giving money to the Nazi party, or at least to certain Nazis. None of this, however, should be allowed to obscure the central fact that the great majority of Germany's big businessmen had neither wanted a Nazi triumph nor contributed materially to it.

The last statement, it should be emphasized, does not necessarily apply to the German business community as a whole. There are, in fact, indications that Hitler received considerable support from small- and middle-sized business.[51] This is not surprising, for it was there that the real and potential entrepreneurial victims of the Great Depression were to be found. The giant businesses of the country knew from past experience that their importance to the national economy was so great that no government could afford to let them go bankrupt; in fact, the cabinets of the republic repeatedly came to the aid of ailing big business concerns rather than face the sharp increase in unemployment that their collapse would entail.[52] Smaller,

---

[51]Two recent studies show this to have been the case during the Nazi party's early years: Georg Franz-Willing, *Die Hitlerbewegung: Der Ursprung 1919-1922* (Hamburg, 1962), 177-98; Werner Maser, *Die Frühgeschichte der NSDAP: Hitlers Weg bis 1924* (Frankfurt a.M., 1965), 396-412. A study written at the time and based on the business press concluded that the same pattern had characterized the last years before 1933: Ernst Lange, "Die politische Ideologie der deutschen industriellen Unternehmerschaft," doctoral dissertation, University of Greifswald, 1933, 36, 80. This was also the view of Theodor Heuss, *Hitlers Weg: Eine historisch-politische Studie über den Nationalsozialismus* (Stuttgart, 1932), 122.

[52]There is much documentation on this in the papers of the *Reichswirtschaftsministerium,* now located in the *Deutsches Zentralarchiv,* Potsdam.

less visible firms could expect no such protection from the abrasive mechanisms of cyclical contraction; for their owners and managers, economic extinction was a real possibility, with the consequence that they were often genuinely desperate men. But the fact nevertheless remains that these small- and middle-sized businessmen can by no stretch of the imagination be included in the ranks of German big business, or, to use Marxist terminology, "the monopoly capitalists." Therefore, unless one is willing to accept the simplistic *cui bono* approach, according to which the eventual economic beneficiaries of Hitler's acquisition of power must necessarily have supported him beforehand, or the sophistic distinction between subjective and objective roles in history that is so popular in Marxist circles, it must be concluded that during its rise to power National Socialism was, in socioeconomic terms, primarily a movement not of winners in the capitalist struggle for survival but of losers and those who feared becoming losers.

It can, of course, be argued that even if the big businessmen did not support Hitler, National Socialism was nevertheless a product of capitalism. Certainly the deprivation and anxiety occasioned by the downward turn of the capitalist economic cycle after 1929 heightened the susceptibility of many Germans to the panaceas offered by the Nazis. The country's capitalist economic system also fostered and exacerbated the class animosities that the Nazis exploited and promised to eliminate. It spawned as well the other long-term economic and social problems to which Nazism was in large measure a response, although a response that offered mainly quack remedies and flights from reality rather than real solutions. National Socialism was thus undeniably a child of the capitalist order. Still, care must be taken not to attach undue significance to that fact. Only a few capitalist societies have produced phenomena comparable to Nazism; on the other hand, the latter shares its capitalist parentage with every other political movement that has emerged from modern Europe, including liberal democracy and Communism.

FRIEDRICH MEINECKE
The Leadership Principle

Friedrich Meinecke in his *The German Catastrophe* introduces a variation on the "Hero in History" theme. He suggests that the sudden loss of the war created a mood in the German people which ran toward a neurotic response to any crisis. The bitterness generated by reparations and the French invasion of the Ruhr strengthened the mood, and impelled Hitler to focus the frustrated fury into a political and social movement. The economic crisis after 1930 was sufficient to join a majority of the people to a program they could not have supported in a saner time.

IN THE RELATIONSHIP between the chance personality and the general tendencies there are endless variations. Quickly they become more separate but never completely separate; quickly they melt inseparably together. Now one factor is stronger, and now the other. Sometimes things seem necessarily to run their course in such a way that nothing at all depends on the individual. But then again an individual intervenes with monstrous vehemence of effect. In everything we may call chance there lies something of the general tendency, and in every general tendency something of chance. In the course of the First World War and in the necessary creation of the Weimar Republic general forces were dominant—for the most part any of the individuals who were here active could have been replaced by someone else who would have done about the same thing. But then came the monstrous effect of Hitler's personality upon already existing general tendencies, which consequently increased enormously and could almost be regarded as his most personal creation. The general tendencies existed in the shape of the currents of rage and despair, and often also the wild readiness for action, which, when Hitler appeared, were already welling up in all classes discontented with the Weimar creation. He needed various fighting aims of a general character to which he could point and through which he could raise to the boiling point the blood of his followers. These aims were the Versailles Treaty and the conditions created by it, then the Jewish question, and finally the economic crisis and unemployment of the late twenties. Without the preexistence of these three complexes Hitler's influence would have been incomprehensible. In a period of quiet the seriously psychopathic individual and the unsuccessful artist would probably have lived his problematical existence to one side somewhere or other. But upon the stage of history the times which were out of joint excited the personality that was out of joint to a mutual and most fearful degree.

JOSEPH GOEBBELS
Personal Magnetism

The following excerpts from *The Early Goebbels Diaries, 1925-1926* illustrate the point made in the foregoing selection from Meinecke. It is difficult for us to accept the idea that a mature and intelligent man could so passionately deify Hitler. Yet Goebbels, who became Minister of Propaganda, was merely expressing what many Germans experienced.

24th July 1926

IN THE MORNING to the Hochlenzer. The chief talks about race questions. It is impossible to reproduce what he said. It must be experienced. He is a genius. The natural, creative instrument of a fate determined by God. I am deeply moved. He is like a child: kind, good, merciful. Like a cat: cunning, clever, agile. Like a lion: roaring and great and gigantic. A fellow, a man. He talks about the state. In the afternoon about winning over the state and the political revolution. Thoughts which I may well have had, but never yet put into words. After supper we go on sitting in the garden of the naval hostel, and he goes on for a long time preaching about the new state and how we are going to fight for it. It sounds like prophecy. Up in the skies a white cloud takes on the shape of the swastika. There is a blinking light that cannot be a star. A sign of fate?! We go back late! The lights of Salzburg shine in the distance. I am indeed happy. This life is worth living. "My head will not roll in the sand until I have

From Helmut Heiber, ed., *The Early Goebbels Diaries, 1925-1926,* trans. by Oliver Watson (New York: Frederick A. Praeger, 1963), p. 100.

completed my mission." Those were his last words. That's what he is like! Indeed! I cannot go to sleep for a long time! The fair woman gave no sign!

25th July 1926

Sunday! We amble a short distance down the path, sit on a bench, and then he tells about 9th November. The Germanic tragedy. Ludendorff acted like a child. The chief is a cunning dog! What followed must not be written about yet. The afternoon we spend in his room and have a natter. He spoils me like a child. The kind friend and master! Outside it is pouring. And Hitler talks! In the evening: he speaks about the country's future architecture and is nothing but an architect. And he fills in the picture by describing the new German constitution: and then he is the master of statecraft! Farewell, my Obersalzberg! These days have signposted my road! A star shines leading me from deep misery! I am his to the end. My last doubts have disappeared. Germany will live! *Heil Hitler!*

26th July 1926

We walk downhill. He walks with me alone. And he talks to me as a father talks to his son. About his war service at the front. And always sketching life with bold strokes. Life's master.

Neurotic Deification

That such views as those expressed in Goebbels' personal diary were routinely published and read is exemplified by the following selections from major publications of leading Nazis.

How shall I give expression, my Fuehrer, to what is in our hearts? How shall I find words for your deeds? Has there ever been a mortal as beloved as you, my Fuehrer? Was there ever belief as strong as the belief in your mission? God sent you to us for Germany.

(Hermann Goering, Munich, 1938)

From Office of the United States Chief of Counsel for Prosecution of Axis Criminality, *Nazi Conspiracy and Aggression* (8 vols; Washington: United States Government Printing Office, 1946), IV, 1106-1107.

Above all was God's hand which has visibly guided the Fuehrer and his Movement. Only those who have no faith, claim that chance has persecuted us. In reality Moltke's word was proven to be true in regard to the Fuehrer and the Party; namely, that in the long run only the strong will have good luck. What had been prepared quietly and had grown organically during ten years, swept over all of Germany like a torrent on 30 January 1933 and during the time which followed. There was nobody in the country and in the world who could have escaped the powerful, resounding rhythm of these events. It was as if a whole people awoke from its sleep, threw off in one quick move the chains which oppressed it and rose like a Phoenix out of the ashes of a fallen system. And out of the flame and enthusiasm with which the masses of millions of people yielded to Hitler and his idea, the cry which once before at the time of the crusades had made Germany rise, seemed to come again: "It is God's will!"

And as he gave us his blessing, he denied it to the others. Although they called for him loudly from their pulpits and party-seats, their work was not his work, their faith was not his faith and their will not his will.

It is not mere chance that millions in Germany are of the holy conviction that National Socialism is more than politics, that in it the word and the will of God proclaim itself, that the bulwark it has created against Bolshevism was conceived on higher aspiration as the last salvation of Occidental culture before the threat of Asiatic atheism.

(Joseph Goebbels, 1934)

It is with pride that we see that one man is kept above all criticism—that is the Fuehrer.

The reason is that everyone feels and knows: he was always right and will always be right. The National Socialism of us all is anchored in the uncritical loyalty, in the devotion to the Fuehrer that does not ask for the wherefore in the individual case, in the tacit performance of his commands. We believe that the Fuehrer is fulfilling a divine mission to German destiny! This belief is beyond challenge.

(Rudolf Hess, Munich, 1928)

SOLOMON BLOOM
The Peasant Caesar

Solomon Bloom in "The Peasant Caesar" refers to the charismatic effect Hitler had on people. But Bloom is more interested in studying Hitler's way of thinking than in studying its effect on others. He concludes that three features emerge in Hitler's mentality, his literalness, an obsession with cunning, and a preference for the rural.

IT IS CLEAR that Hitler was not "standard." We cannot infer his attitudes and ideas from his social position or ambitions, his way of living, or his image of himself. To get at his mentality, we must watch it unfolding in his decisions and deeds, in *Mein Kampf,* in his myriad speeches, and in informal and unguarded remarks. In his last years he unbuttoned himself to his intimate circle in interminable after-dinner *causerie,* which was duly recorded for posterity by secretaries and edited by associates in the *Tischgesprache* (Bonn, 1952). As one winnows this vast mass—a sad chaffy and gritty mass—three features emerge.

For the most important of these it is difficult to find an apt expression. I shall call it *literalness.* Hitler was unable to grasp any meaning except in its literal sense. He lacked that capacity for perceiving nuance and shading which marks the cultivated man. He lacked the feeling for metaphor and the figurative without which only the most palpable phenomena can be perceived. Hitler's mind was the opposite of the poetic. What was generalization or approximation to others was inflexible law to him. That politics and diplomacy are often fed by half-truths and untruths; that force plays a large role in domestic and international success; that peoples may be distinguished by differences of culture or skill, are considerations that are usually subjected to discount and modification in judging particular cases. Hitler's mind translated them into the propositions that all politicians are, and ought to be, *nothing* but barefaced liars; that success in international affairs is based on *nothing but* force and cunning; and that, while a few peoples are creative, all others are not only inferior to them but hardly distinguishable from animals. . . .

From Solomon Bloom, "The Peasant Caesar," *Commentary,* XXIII, (May, 1957.), 406-418. Reprinted from *Commentary* by permission; Copyright © 1957 by the American Jewish Committee.

Hitler's chief psychological trait was an obsession with cunning. He read the history of civilization as a triumph of craft. The advances and inventions that raised man above the animals boiled down to a string of "tricks and ruses" by which the highest races circumvented and exploited nature, the animal world and the inferior races. Further progress rested similarly upon the strategic enslavement of men. International success began and ended with wile. Hermann Rauschning suggested to Hitler that two could play at that game. "Trickery invited counter-trickery: 'Maybe,' replied Hitler, 'but anyhow I get there first.'" Hitler's opponents were all foxes, but he would outfox them. If the Marxists have discovered the means of enticing the masses, he has discovered their discovery and will beat them at their own game. If the British have built an empire by the crafty exercise of violence, Hitler, alone of all their rivals, has penetrated their mystery and will turn their own methods against them. The Jews have used the theory of the "chosen people," and have drawn strength from their very dispersion. He would do the same: he would raise the Germans to be an elect people and use the ethnic Germans in all parts of the world to second his aims. The simulation of "socialism" on a larger scale; the duplication of a more compact and extensive British empire; the facsimile of the "Elders of Zion" in an even cleverer form—that is the "New Order." Hitler was the "hick" who outsmarted the city "slickers." His "idea" was a composite counterfeit of the "secrets" of his enemies and rivals.

If the psychology was crafty and the mentality literal, the content was splashed with predilections and images stemming from the village and the small town. Bucolic pictures spring spontaneously to Hitler's mind. When he wished to say that community was not based on natural instincts and that only force created society, he was reminded that when, in his native haunts, the farm boys and servants met at the local inn they always got to quarreling and fighting with knives. They were welded into a "society only when the gendarmes came on the scene." To justify sexual intercourse and childbearing out of wedlock, he recalled that in his rural Austria no peasant would marry a woman who had not already proved fertile and capable of giving birth to healthy children.

Through Hitler's speeches and writings there runs a strong undercurrent of antagonism to urban and cosmopolitan civilization. He was for some years a derelict in the great city of Vienna; he never became a confident citizen of it. He always extolled the countrified Munichs and Linzes, the Weimars and Bayreuths above the Viennas and Berlins. Even in his days of power, he preferred his country retreats to the German capital. In former centuries, he remarked, the towns were centers of culture and art, but the modern city was merely an accidental place of temporary settlement. . . .

A nation, he shouted, can exist without cities, but not without peasants. The cities themselves are replenished with country blood. The peasant "may be primitive but he is healthy." He is a sound heathen, while the bohemian only pretends to heathenism. . . .

Land- and peasant-mindedness, cunning, and literalness—these were the attributes of Hitler's mind. They do not add up to a complete portrait. To finish it one would have to describe Hitler's sinuous opportunism when out of power, his brutality and tenacity, his insight into political psychology and propaganda, his oratorical energies, and his quality of obsession and hypnosis. Nor do the trait that we have sketched go far to explain the rise of Nazism, however much they may explain of its denouement. They do not account fully for Hitler's policy during his first years in office, when his power was hedged by severe domestic and international limits. . . .

Hitler's literal reading of evolutionary law, combined with his brutality, account for the immolation of whole peoples and the criminal "experiments" with individuals. The extermination of the Jews and other groups cannot be put down merely to political opportunism or to the search for scapegoats. The exterminations were begun in 1942, when the Jews had exhausted their role as scapegoats, and they gathered in intensity and volume as the fortunes of the war turned against Germany. Hitler was determined to snatch a "racial" victory from the jaws of military defeat, feeling, quite correctly, that he could commit under the cover of war mass murders that would be difficult, if not impossible, in peace. War was, to him, the great racial revolution. It exalted the strong, and devoured the weak.

It has often been argued that he could have made good his conquest of Western Russia by coming to terms with the Ukranians. This was certainly common sense, but his territorial plans and his hopes for a refreshed German peasantry and nobility made a compromise impossible, since they required the decimation and abasement of the Slavs. The nationality policy of the Third Reich in Russia was not a "mistake" of judgment or tactics; it followed "unalterably" from Hitler's purpose and methods.

Finally, his reliance on cunning explains how he deceived, and eventually antagonized, the great powers. On his theory that diplomacy was mere deception, he could not believe that the British would enter the war in 1939 or that, having entered it, they would fight seriously. If they did, the war would spread to two fronts, and the two-front war was the principal score on which he attacked, and mocked endlessly, the former imperial regime of Germany. The British called his bluff instead of countering it with another, as they were expected to do.

Such were the consequences of Hitler's outlook. What was its inspiration and source, where its local habitation?

Was it Germany? Certainly Hitlerism found a powerful echo in German traditions, institutions, and movements. Hitler's literalness met its more sophisticated foster brothers in German pedantry, narrow specialization, and blinkered expertise. Led by the primitivist doctrinaire, technologists and "scientists" who could not detect, with their finest instruments, the difference between vivisection and murder, between experiment and crime, produced the most dreadful holocaust in history. Hitler's chicanery appealed to a people that for two generations had worshipped a Bismarck. Diplomatic deception fertilized the old military machine and the professional General Staff and drove them to achieve remarkable if inconclusive victories. Hitler's insistence on territorial power struck a sensitive chord in the heart of the Junkers. His bent for the natural, the rustic, and the pagan reinforced the romantic youth ideologies and movements that abounded in Germany: the hikers, the solstice-celebrants, the Nordic and nudist enthusiasts, the sex orgiasts. Without these passions, without the Prussian instruments, without the invertebracy of the ubiquitous German expert, Hitlerism could not have got very far. Germany, and not Hitler, is responsible for the success of Hitlerism. . . .

Hitler thus played a double role. He promised to satisfy the aspirations of German imperialism and militarism, and so obtained control over the German army and economy. He gave expression to the hatred for Western ideas which had nourished reaction in Eastern Europe for generations, and so foisted German dominion upon it. The resentment and ambition that delivered Eastern Europe and Germany into Hitler's hands at the same time blinded them to the real price he proposed eventually to exact of them. Germany craved that leading role in Western society and civilization which states like Great Britain and France had held in the past. Instead, she got a kind of Oriental barbarism that even Oriental despots had long abandoned. The difference between what Germany herself desired and what she tried to foist upon the world through Hitler is the reason for the lingering confusion in the German mind over the meaning of the Nazi experience. Much of the nature of the German catastrophe is explained by its incoherence.

The price Hitler meant to exact of Eastern Europe was, of course, higher than that he demanded of Germany. Eastern Europe he would use as a hammer to beat Western Europe into submission—and then melt down the hammer. He would destroy the best part of the peoples of Eastern Europe and make primitive slaves of the rest. In the end, Hitler deceived his allies—and his own people—much more than he did his enemies.

It was as if, after the First World War, German imperialism and Eastern reaction had shouted their wrath and resentment into a vast abyss. A single echo answered them—Adolf Hitler.

ADOLF HITLER
Master of Propaganda

Hitler probably made better use of propaganda than any other world leader. He understood the German people and what they wanted to hear. He also knew how to convince the Germans that he had the answers they wanted. The following two selections from *Mein Kampf* illustrate Hitler's thinking on the use of propaganda.

To whom should propaganda be addressed? To the scientifically trained intelligentsia or to the less educated masses?

It must be addressed always and exclusively to the masses. . . . The function of propaganda does not lie in the scientific training of the individual, but in calling the masses' attention to certain facts, processes, necessities, etc., whose significance is thus for the first time placed within their field of vision.

The whole art consists in doing this so skillfully that everyone will be convinced that the fact is real, the process necessary, the necessity correct, etc. But since propaganda is not and cannot be the

From Adolf Hitler, *Mein Kampf,* trans. by Ralph Manheim (Boston: Houghton Mifflin, 1943), pp. 179-180, 231-232.

necessity in itself, since its function, like the poster, consists in attracting the attention of the crowd, and not in educating those who are already educated or who are striving after education and knowledge, its effect for the most part must be aimed at the emotions and only to a very limited degree at the so-called intellect. All propaganda must be popular and its intellectual level must be adjusted to the most limited intelligence among those it is addressed to. Consequently, the greater the mass it is intended to reach, the lower its purely intellectual level will have to be. But if, as in propaganda for sticking out a war, the aim is to influence a whole people, we must avoid excessive intellectual demands on our public, and too much caution cannot be exerted in this direction.

The more modest its intellectual ballast, the more exclusively it takes into consideration the emotions of the masses, the more effective it will be. And this is the best proof of the soundness or unsoundness of a propaganda campaign, and not success in pleasing a few scholars or young aesthetes. . . .

The receptivity of the great masses is very limited, their intelligence is small, but their power of forgetting is enormous.

. . . The magnitude of a lie always contains a factor of credibility, since the great masses of the people in the very bottom of their hearts tend to be corrupted rather than consciously and purposely evil, and that, therefore, in view of the primitive simplicity of their mind, they more easily fall a victim to a big lie than to a little one, since they themselves lie in little things, but would be ashamed of lies that were too big. Such a falsehood would never enter their heads, and they will not be able to believe in the possibility of such monstrous effrontery and infamous misrepresentation in others; yes, even when enlightened on the subject, they will long doubt and waver, and continue to accept at least one of these causes as true. Therefore, something of even the most insolent lie will always remain and stick—a fact which all the great lie-virtuosi and lying-clubs in this world know only too well and also make the most treacherous use of.

IV Consolidation of Power

The election of March 5, 1933, gave the Nazis 288 seats in the Reichstag, or 44% of the 647 total seats. With the support of the Nationalists, Hitler could depend on a clear majority for a normal democratic process of government. But Hitler had come to the Chancellorship on a platform of opposition to the democratic process and a promise of totalitarian government. He had no thought of operating a parliamentary government. Every activity of the party, then, from January 30 on was directed toward the passage of an enabling act which would provide totalitarian power. The methods were based on terrorism. The burning of the Reichstag building provided sufficient excuse to arrest the entire Communist delegation of 81 members, and that action served as the basis for frightening the other delegations into voting democracy out of existence.

Three days after the first meeting of the new Reichstag, Hitler introduced his enabling act, and it was passed by a vote of 441 to 94. This vote of the democratically elected representatives of the German people marks the end of democracy and the beginning of a totalitarian regime. Hitler moved quickly to consolidate his power by a whole series of decrees which brought all institutions and individuals under an authoritarian dictatorship. When he purged his own party of all possible opponents to his dictatorship and decreed his own presidency without a ripple of opposition, his power was complete.

ERICH EYCK
Hitler Becomes Chancellor

The following selection from Erich Eyck's *A History of the Weimar Republic* depicts Hitler's appointment as Chancellor on 30 January 1933.

ON THE EVENING of this Monday, January 30, 1933, as the news of Hitler's appointment spread throughout the city, an endless line of his triumphant supporters, waving torches and singing the Horst Wessel song, paraded through the Wilhelmstrasse. Field Marshall von Hindenburg, half mystified, half astonished, and utterly confused, gazed down at the crowds that waved at him politely, crowds which he had never really known. Only the military marches stirred an echo in his weary old brain.

Hitler, on the other hand, stood in the window of his Chancellery greeting his "brown battalions marching": the SA, the SS, the Hitler Youth, and the thousands of his other supporters who were ecstatically celebrating his victory. The Austrian gazed down at them with the beaming smile of a man who, having accomplished the impossible, had achieved the goal of his demonic ambition.

The attempt by the German people to rule themselves had failed. A time now came when Germany ceased to be a state based on law. This was the time when German judges allowed their courtrooms to be overrun by the mob who drove out the people whose noses they did not like; when the judges saw their independence and security abolished and their professional advancement become dependent on the way their decisions pleased the ruling party; when the judges let the leader of that party declare as law whatever served the interests of the Volk—as he determined those interests.

It was the time when Themis, goddess of Justice, had the blindfold ripped from her eyes in order that she might determine the precise ethnic origin and political opinion of every party in the disputes over which she presided; the time when a German minister of justice found it "lawful" that the Chancellor of Germany should have his political opponents slaughtered by the hundreds without the slightest semblance of a trial and should use this convenient opportunity to have some of his earlier adversaries murdered.

It was the time when Germany became the most frightful example of Augustine's admonition, "Without justice, what are states if not great bands of thieves?"; when Germans demonstrated the meaning of Bismarck's statement that they liked so well to quote, "We Germans fear God and nothing else in the whole world," by setting fire to the house of God and by quivering before every Nazi clerk; when freedom of thought was replaced by "coordination," and personal liberty, by concentration camps to which thousands upon thousands were arbitrarily dragged and where they were exposed to all the torments which a laughing brutality could devise, while their fellow Germans—who, at the theater, were always so deeply moved by the Prisoners' Chorus in *Fidelio*—did not lose a night's sleep over the tortures and injustice which these real prisoners suffered daily.

It was the time when this nation, whose greatest poet had written a German *Iphigenie* memorializing *Gastrecht,* the honored rights of the harbored guest, now observed the customs of hospitality by expelling thousands of German Jews from their own fatherland, people whose fathers and fathers' fathers had lived and worked on German soil for generations but who were now called strangers, *Gastvolk,* by their German rulers because the brutish hate of an alien tyrant demanded this persecution; the time when Germans watched without concern as those who had not found foreign refuge soon enough were carted away into slavery to be murdered in gas chambers or in "experiments"; the time when little children were torn from their weeping mothers and sent to die in some unknown corner of the East.

It was the time when the word "German" became a symbol of everything humanity condemns as brutal, outrageous, and base.

All this started on Monday, January 30, 1933. And young Germans waved their torches in delight.

The Enabling Act

The appointment of Hitler as Chancellor of Germany in January 1933 did not establish a dictatorship. Not until the passage of the Enabling Act on 24 March 1933 did the representatives of the German people vote away democracy and vote in a totalitarian government.

THE REICHSTAG has resolved upon the following law which is promulgated herewith with approval of the Reichsrat after it has been established that all the requirements of legislation for changing the constitution have been complied with.

SECTION 1

Laws for the Reich can be resolved upon also by the Reich Cabinet besides the procedure provided by the constitution of the Reich. This also applies to the laws pursuant to sections 85 subsection 2 and 87 of the Reich-Constitution.

SECTION 2

The laws for the Reich resolved upon by the Reich Cabinet may deviate from the Reich-Constitution so far as they do not deal with the institution of the Reichstag or the Reichsrat as such. The powers of the Reich-President will remain intact.

SECTION 3

The laws for the Reich resolved upon by the Reich-Cabinet are issued by the Reich-Chancellor and promulgated in the Reichsgesetz-blatt. They will become effective, so far as they do not determine otherwise on the day following their promulgation. Section 68 and 77 of the Reich-Constitution are not applicable to the laws resolved upon by the Reich-Cabinet.

SECTION 4

Treaties of the Reich with foreign countries relating to matters of the legislation of the Reich do not require the approval of the bodies participating in the legislation. The Reich-Cabinet issues the rules necessary for the execution of such treaties.

From Office of United States Chief of Counsel for Prosecution of Axis Criminality, *Nazi Conspiracy and Aggression* (8 vols; Washington: United States Government Printing Office, 1946), IV, 638-639.

Section 5

This law will become effective on the day of its promulgation. It becomes ineffective on 1 April 1937. Moreover it becomes ineffective if the present Reich-Cabinet should be replaced by another. Berlin, 24 March 1933

The Reich-President
von Hindenburg
The Reich-Chancellor
Adolf Hitler
The Reich-Minister for the Interior
Frick
The Reich-Minister for Foreign Affairs
Freiherr von Neurath
The Reich-Minister for Finances
Count Schwerin von Krosigk

Legalization of Terror

Adolf Hitler strengthened his dictatorship with a series of decrees to restrict the freedoms of the German people. All of those decrees were possible because of the dictatorial powers that the Enabling Act had given to Hitler. The first of these acts justifies the use of terror tactics against the Communist and Socialist parties.

I declared at that time before thousands of fellow Germans, each bullet which leaves the barrel of a police pistol now, is my bullet. If one calls this murder, then I have murdered; I ordered all this, I back it up; I assume the responsibility, and I am not afraid to do so.

Through a network of outer offices converging into the headquarters in Berlin, I am daily, one could almost say hourly, informed about everything that happens in widespread Prussia.

We had to deal ruthlessly with these enemies of the state. It must

From Office of United States Chief of Counsel for Prosecution of Axis Criminality, *Nazi Conspiracy and Aggression* (8 vols; Washington: United States Government Printing Office, 1946), IV, 1033.

not be forgotten that at the moment of our seizure of power over 6 million people officially voted for communism and about 8 million for marxism in the Reichstag elections in March.

Thus the concentration camps were created, to which we had to send first all the thousands of functionaries of the Communist and Social Democratic parties.

The Gestapo deserves a great deal of credit for the success of the revolution and for the consolidation of its achievements. Right in the middle of this constructive work, occurred the blaze that destroyed the high cupola and the auditorium of the Reichstag. Criminal hands had set this fire, had put the German Reichstag in flames, in order to give a last beacon to dying Communism, so that it could make one last desperate thrust before the Hitler government was consolidated. The blaze was to be the signal for the Communist party for general terror, for a general uprising and for civil war. That it did not have these consequences, Germany and the world owe not to the noble motives of Communism, but solely to the iron resolution and the hard fist of Adolf Hitler and his closest collaborators, who struck more quickly than the enemy had expected, and harder than he could imagine, and with the first blow suppressed Communism once and for all.

That night, when I ordered the arrest of 4,000 Communist functionaries, I knew that by dawn Communism had lost a great battle.

Against the Jews

Order Number 5 was the beginning of discrimination against the Jews. The order informed the public which businesses Jews owned.

CONCERNING the defensive action against the Jewish horror and boycott agitation beginning Saturday, 1 April at 10 AM, the local action committees are again reminded to see to it most strictly:

1. That any use of force is to be avoided, establishments cannot be

From Office of United States Chief of Counsel for Prosecution of Axis Criminality, *Nazi Conspiracy and Aggression* (8 vols; Washington:United States Government Printing Office, 1946), IV, 760-761.

closed by the committee or by its agents. On the other hand, closing by the proprietor himself is not to be prevented.

Entering of Jewish establishments is strictly forbidden to SA or SS members or other agents of the action committee.

The only duty of the defensive guards is to inform the public that the proprietor of the establishment is a Jew.

2. That boycotting of establishments is refrained from if it has not been definitely proved that the proprietor is a Jew.

3. That provocateurs cause no property damage which is counter to the purpose of the defensive action.

4. That the action committee be kept informed of all details of the course of the defensive action by the SA and SS controllers so as to be constantly well posted.

5. Posters with provocative contents are forbidden.

Central Committee for defense against the
Jewish horror and boycott agitation
STREICHER

The Organization of Labor

The End of the Marxist Class Struggle placed the largest trade union in Germany, the German Trade Union, under the leadership of the Nazi party. The Union now could do nothing without the approval of the Nazi party.

BUT AS YET the trade associations of the German working class, the representative bodies of workers and employees, were in the hands of Marxist leaders, who did not guide the German labor movement for the benefit of the working German people, but only considered it as the shock troop of their crazy international Marxist class-struggle ideology.

National Socialism, which today has assumed leadership of the German working class, can no longer bear the responsibility for leaving the men and women of the German working class, the members of the largest trade organization in the world, the German

From Office of the United States Chief of Counsel for Prosecution of Axis Criminality, *Nazi Conspiracy and Aggression* (8 vols; Washington: United States Government Printing Office, 1946), IV, 864-866.

Trade Union movement, in the hands of people who do not know a fatherland that is called Germany. Because of that, the National Socialist Factory Cell Organization [NSBO] has taken over the leadership of the trade unions. The NSBO has eliminated the old leadership of the Trade Unions of the AGDB [General German Trade Union League] and of the AFA [General Independent Employees' Federation].

New German labor leaders have replaced senile wardheelers [*verkalkte Bonzen*]. The proven pioneers of the National Socialist Factory Cell Organization [NSBO], who have fought to the limit for the rights of German labor from the beginning, have taken over the leadership of the trade union associations. That proves that the struggle of National Socialism is not directed against the trade union idea as such, but only against the bureaucratized leaderships, because they are the foes of the German labor movement. The old, painstakingly attained rights of the workers' and employees' associations will not be touched. On the contrary, the new National Socialist trade union leadership will make good the harm inflicted on the German working class by class struggle and internationalism.

On 2 May 1933 the National Socialist Factory Cell Organization took over the leadership of all trade unions, all trade union buildings were occupied and most stringent control has been organized over financial and personnel matters of the organizations.

The leadership of the Action Committee for the Protection of German Labor has been assumed by Party Member Dr. Ley, Deputy: Schmeer.

The leadership of the General German Trade Union League has been taken over by Party Member Schumann. Party Member Muchow takes care of the fundamental questions of organization. Party Member Biallas is responsible for press and propaganda.

Party Member Peppler assumes leadership of the Genral Independent Employees' Federation [AFA].

Party Member Peppler assumes leadership of the General Independent Employees' Federation [AFA].

Auditing has been taken over by Party Member Brinkmann.

German workers and employees! Help us to build a new Germany of national liberty and socialist justice. Help to transform the trade unions to the media of fruitful work. Maintain discipline, then your work will be accompanied by success, to the benefit of the entire German people, but primarily of German workers and employees.

The new National Socialist trade union leadership will attempt to make good the damage done to the German working class by class struggle and internationalism. We appeal to the entire German people, to trade union members of all shades and associations.

Have confidence in the proven fighters of the National Socialist Factory Cell Organization!

Attempts at sabotage by unscrupulous mischief-makers will be avenged with the whole severity of the law. Comply with all future directives, it is a matter of your and your children's future!

Now to work!
Long live Socialism!
Long live Germany!

The Organization of Students

The following law (April 22, 1933) declared that only students of German descent represented the student body at a scientific university. A Jew was not considered to be of German descent.

THE GOVERNMENT of the Reich has decreed the following law which is promulgated herewith:

SECTION 1

Students of German descent and mother tongue, fully registered with a scientific University shall constitute the Student-body of such University, regardless of their citizenship:

SECTION 2

The Student-body is a part of the University and represents the students as a whole. It shall be instrumental in ensuring that students fulfill their duties towards the people, the State, and the University.

From Office of United States Chief of Counsel for Prosecution of Axis Criminality, *Nazi Conspiracy and Aggression* (8 vols; Washington: United States Government Printing Office, 1946), IV, 718.

SECTION 3

Details relating to organization and work of the student-bodies will be determined by Land Governments' Student Regulations and by the by-laws of the Universities and the Student-bodies.

Berlin, 22 April 1933

The Reich Chancellor
ADOLF HITLER

The Reich Minister of the Interior
FRICK

The Organization of the Youth Leagues

All Youth Leagues in Germany were dissolved by the following act. Any Youth League had to clear with the Youth Leader of the German Reich before it could organize.

IMPORTANT ORDER OF BALDUR VON SCHIRACH

NSK Berlin, 22 June
The Youth Leader of the German Reich, Baldur von Schirach, has published the following order:

* * *

ORDER 2

1. The Greater German League [*Grossdeutscher Bund*], together with its sub-and member organizations, is dissolved as of 17 June 1933. The property of the Greater German League and of the affiliated sub-and member organizations is to be secured. Thus,

---

From Office of United States Chief of Counsel for Prosecution of Axis Criminality, *Nazi Conspiracy and Aggression* (8 vols; Washington: United States Government Printing Office, 1946), IV, 870-871.

along with the Greater German League the following have been dissolved:

1. Free Band of the Young Nation [*Freischar Junger Nation*].
2. German Free Band [*Deutsche Freischar*].
3. German Boy Scout League [*Deutscher Pfadfinderbund*].
4. The Geusses [*Die Geusen*].
5. Community Circle of German Boy Scouts [*Ringgemeinschaft deutscher Pfadfinder*].
6. Circle of German Boy Scout Districts [*Ring deutscher Pfadfindergaue*].
7. German Boy Scout Corps [*Deutsches Pfadfinderkorps*].
8. Free Band of Protestant Boy Scouts [*Freischar evangelischer Pfadfinder*].

2. The Reich Committee of German Youth Associations [*Reichsausschuss der deutschen Jugendverbaende*] is dissolved herewith. Previous tasks of the Reich Committee will be taken over into the expanded sphere of tasks of the Youth Leadership of the German Reich.

3. All Youth Organizations in Germany are to be reported to the Youth Leader of the German Reich (Berlin NW 40, 10, Kronprinzenufer, Department for Organizations). Youth Organizations which have not reported, or reported only incompletely, by 15 July 1933, are to be considered as dissolved. It is expressly emphasized that the term "Youth Organizations" also comprises such organizations which are groups within adult organizations. The reports are to be submitted by the top leadership of individual youth organizations for the entire organization. Insofar as the youth groups of adult organizations do not have centralized youth leadership, the leadership of the adult organization is obligated to submit the report.

It is mandatory that the report contain:

1. name of the society (with accurate information about the legal status of the society);
2. board of directors of the society (accurate information about name, residence, and telephone number (if applicable);
3. information relative to person authorized to represent the society;
4. office of the society (telephone);
5. banking and postal checking accounts of the society, with indication who is authorized to sign for the society there;
6. accurate membership figures with indication when the figures were ascertained;

7. statutes of the society;
8. information about the organizational structure of the society, insofar as they are not contained in the statutes;
9. information about chairmen of districts, regions, states, or similar subdivisions;

4. The tasks of the Youth Leader of the German Reich must be accomplished partially with the help of contributions of affiliated organizations. The amount of contributions will be fixed in the very near future.

Law Against the New Establishment of Parties

The law against the establishment of parties (July 14, 1933) outlawed all political parties except the Nazi party.

THE GERMAN CABINET has resolved the following law, which is herewith promulgated:

1. The National Socialist German Workers' Party constitutes the only political party in Germany.

2. Whoever undertakes to maintain the organizational structure of another political party or to form a new political party will be punished with penal servitude up to three years or with imprisonment of from six months to three years, if the deed is not subject to a greater penalty according to other regulations.

Berlin, July 14, 1933

> Reich's Chancellor Adolf Hitler
> Reich's Minister of the Interior Frick
> Reich's Minister of Justice Gürtner

From Office of United States Chief of Counsel for Prosecution of Axis Criminality, *Nazi Conspiracy and Aggression* (8 vols; Washington: United States Government Printing Office, 1946), III, 962.

Press Censorship

The Editorial Law (October 4, 1933) provided for censorship of the press. It also determined who qualified to be editor of a newspaper.

THE REICH GOVERNMENT has resolved upon the following law, which is hereby published:

PART ONE
The Editorial Profession

SECTION 1

The cooperative work carried on as main employment or based upon appointment to the position of chief editor in the shaping of the intellectual contents by written word, dissemination of news or pictures of the newspapers or political periodicals, which are published within the area of the Reich, is a public task, which is regulated as to its professional duties and rights by the state through this law. Its bearers are called editors. Nobody may call himself an editor who is not entitled to do so, according to this law.

SECTION 2

(1) Newspapers and periodicals are printed matters which appear in regular sequence at intervals of at most 3 months, without limiting their circulation to a certain group of persons.

(2) All reproductions of writings or illustrations, destined for dissemination, which are produced by means of a mass reproduction process are to be considered as printed matter.

SECTION 3

(1) The provisions of this law relating to newspapers are valid also for political periodicals.

From Office of United States Chief of Counsel for Prosecution of Axis Criminality, *Nazi Conspiracy and Aggression* (8 vols; Washington: United States Government Printing Office, 1946), IV, 709-717.

(2) This law does not apply to newspapers and periodicals which are published by official order.

(3) The Reich Minister of Public Enlightenment and Propaganda will determine which periodicals are to be considered as political within the meaning of the law. In case the periodical affects a certain vocational field, he will make the decision in agreement with the highest Reich or State agency concerned.

SECTION 4

Cooperation in the shaping of the intellectual contents of the German newspapers is also considered as such, if it does not take place in the management of a newspaper, but in an establishment, which is to supply newspapers with intellectual contents, (written word, news, or pictures).

PART TWO

Admission to the Profession of Editor

SECTION 5

Persons who can be editors are only those who:

1. possess the German citizenship,
2. have not lost the civic rights [*buergerliche Ehrenrechte*] and the qualification for the tenure of public offices.
3. are of Aryan descent, and are not married to a person of non-Aryan descent,
4. have completed the 21st year of age,
5. are capable of handling business,
6. have been trained in the profession,
7. have the qualities which the task of exerting intellectual influence upon the public requires.

SECTION 13

Editors are charged to treat their subjects truthfully and to judge them according to the best of their knowledge.

SECTION 14

Editors are especially bound to keep out of the newspapers anything which:

1. in any manner is misleading to the public, mixes selfish aims with community aims,

2. tends to weaken the strength of the German Reich, outwardly or inwardly, the common will of the German people, the German defense ability, culture or economy, or offends the religious sentiments of others,

3. offends the honor and dignity of Germany,

4. illegally offends the honor or the welfare of another, hurts his reputation, makes him ridiculous or contemptible,

5. is immoral for other reasons.

SECTION 15

Editors are bound to exercise their profession conscientiously and by their behavior inside or outside their professional activities prove themselves worthy of the respect which this profession demands.

SECTION 19

The editor-in-chief is required to draw up in writing a plan for distribution of work, from which must be evident what part of the tasks of editing are to be taken by each editor and to what extent he has the authority to issue directions to other editors, in accordance with the terms of the contracts of employment and the supplementary directives of the publisher.

SECTION 20

(1) Editors of a newspaper are responsible under professional, criminal and civil law, for its intellectual content so far as they themselves wrote or selected it. The responsibility under criminal or civil law of other persons is not thereby excluded.

(2) The chief editor is responsible for the over-all editorial policy of the newspaper.

(3) The editor-in-chief is required:

(a) to take care that only such contributions are accepted as have been written or selected for acceptance by an editor.

(b) to take care that the first and last names as well as the residence of the editor-in-chief and his deputies, as well as that of each editor to whom a specific part of the direction of a newspaper is delegated, is reported.

(c) upon request to give information to anyone establishing a legal interest therein, as to which editor bears the responsibility for a contribution, so far as this is not evident from the data under subdivision b.

SECTION 21

Editors who cooperate in the shaping of the intellectual contents of a newspaper by their activity with an enterprise of the kind mentioned in Section 4, are responsible for the contents to the extent of their cooperation.

SECTION 31

(1) An editor who fails in his public duties, as set forth in Sections 13 to 15, 19, 20, subsection 3, commits a professional misdemeanor. In such case the Professional Court may:

1. warn the editor,
2. punish him with a fine not exceeding the sum of one month's professional earning,
3. decree the removal of his name from the professional roster.

(2) His license to exercise the editorial profession and to call himself an editor is terminated with such removal.

(3) The Professional Court may temporarily deny an editor, against whom proceedings in an honorary court have been instituted, the right to exercise his profession.

SECTION 35

The Reich Minister for Public Enlightenment and Propaganda may decree the removal of an editor from the professional list independent of the proceedings of the Professional Court, if he deems it necessary for pressing reasons of public welfare.

PART FIVE

Protection of the Editorial Profession
Afforded by the Penal Laws
SECTION 36

Whosoever works as an editor despite the fact he is not registered in the professional rosters, or despite the fact that the exercise of his profession has been prohibited temporarily, will be punished with imprisonment up to one year, or fined.

SECTION 47

The Reich Minister for Public Enlightenment and Propaganda will set the date on which this law becomes valid.
Berlin, October 1933

The Reich Chancellor
ADOLF HITLER
The Reich Minister for Public
Enlightenment and Propaganda
DR. GOEBBELS

Law for the Reconstruction of the Reich

The Law for the Reconstruction of the Reich (January 30, 1934) transferred most of the powers of the Länder [states] to the central government, thus strengthening the hold Hitler had over Germany.

THE POPULAR REFERENDUM and the Reichstag election of November 12, 1933, have proven that the German people have attained an indestructible internal unity superior to all internal subdivisions of political character.

Consequently, the Reichstag has enacted the following law which is hereby promulgated with the unanimous vote of the Reichstag after ascertaining that the requirements of the Reich Constitution have been met:

From Office of United States Chief of Counsel for Prosecution of Axis Criminality, *Nazi Conspiracy and Aggression* (8 vols; Washington: United States Government Printing Office, 1946), IV, 642-643.

ARTICLE I

Popular assemblies [*Volksvertretungen*] of the *Laender* shall be abolished.

ARTICLE II

(1) The sovereign powers [*Hoheitsrechte*] of the *Laender* are transferred to the Reich.
(2) The *Laender* governments are placed under the Reich government.

ARTICLE III

The Reich governors are placed under the administrative supervision of the Reich Minister of Interior.

ARTICLE IV

The Reich Government may issue new constitutional laws.

ARTICLE V

The Reich Minister of Interior may administer the necessary legal and administrative regulations for the execution of the law.

ARTICLE VI

This law shall be effective on the day of its promulgation. Berlin, 30 January 1934.

The Reich President
VON HINDENBURG
The Reich Chancellor
ADOLF HITLER
The Reich Minister of the Interior
FRICK

The Opposition Destroyed

On 30 June 1934 Hitler purged the Nazi party by killing over 1000 supposed loyal Nazis. He issued the following order 3 July 1934 to justify his purge.

THE REICH GOVERNMENT has enacted the following law, which is hereby promulgated:

ONLY ARTICLE

The measures taken on 30 June and 1 and 2 July 1934 to counteract attempt at treason and high treason shall be considered as national emergency defense.

Berlin, 3 July 1934.

The Reich Chancellor
ADOLF HITLER
The Reich Minister of the Interior
FRICK

The Reich Minister of Justice
DR. GUERTNER

From Office of United States Chief of Counsel for Prosecution of Axis Criminality, *Nazi Conspiracy and Aggression* (8 vols; Washington: United States Government Printing Office, 1946), IV, 699.

Chancellor and President

The final act (I August 1934) consolidated the office of President of Germany with that of the Chancellor. This act became effective on the death of President von Hindenburg and gave Hitler control over the two top executive posts in Germany.

THE REICH GOVERNMENT has enacted the following law which is hereby promulgated:

SECTION 1

The office of the Reichspraesident will be consolidated with that of the Reich Chancellor. The existing authority of the Reichspraesident shall consequently be transferred to the Fuehrer and Reich Chancellor, Adolf Hitler. He shall select his representative.

SECTION 2

This law is effective as of the time of the death of Reichspraesident von Hindenburg.

The Reich Chancellor
  Adolf Hitler
The Reich Deputy Chancellor
  von Papen
The Reich Minister of Foreign Affairs
  Freiherr von Neurath
The Reich Minister of Interior
  Frick
The Reich Minister of Finance
  Graf Schwerin von Krosigk
The Reich Minister of Labor
  Franz Seldte
The Reich Minister of Justice
  Dr. Guertner

From Office of United States Chief of Counsel for Prosecution of Axis Criminality, *Nazi Conspiracy and Aggression* (8 vols; Washington: United States Government Printing Office, 1946), IV, 639-640.

The Reich Minister of Defense
von Blomberg
The Reich Postal Minister and Transportation Minister
Freiherr von Eltz
The Reich Minister for Nutrition and Agriculture
R. Walther Darre
The Reich Minister for Enlightenment and Propaganda
Dr. Goebbels
The Reich Minister for Air Travel
Hermann Goering
The Reich Minister for Science, Training and Education
Bernhard Rust
The Reich Minister without Portfolio
Rudolf Hess
The Reich Minister without Portfolio
Hanns Kerrl

Suggestions for Further Reading

In the following bibliographical essay we have aimed to provide an introduction to the literature available to the general reader in most college libraries. Those works from which our selections were taken have been excluded, because complete citations appear with the selection.

For those students interested in further research in the period several special collections will prove useful. Grete Heinz and Agnes F. Peterson (compl.), *NSDAP Hauptarchiv: Guide to the Hoover Institution Microfilm Collection* (Stanford: Hoover Institution on War, Revolution and Peace, 1964), have published a guide to one of the finest collections in existence. A unique collection of documents was compiled in preparation for the trials of Nazi leaders after World War II, and a selection has been published by the International Military Tribunal, *Trial of the Major War Criminals before the International Military Tribunal, Nuremberg, 14 November, 1945-1 October, 1946,* 42 vols. (Nuremberg: International Military Tribunal, 1947). The documents are in German, but some of the most useful have been translated in Office of United States Chief of Counsel for Prosecution of Axis Criminality, *Nazi Conspiracy and Aggression,* 8 vols. (Washington: U.S. Government Printing Office, 1946). Another useful U.S. government publication is *Foreign Relations of the United States; Diplomatic Papers; 1933.*

For the chaos at the end of World War I *Official German Documents Relating to the World War,* translated under the supervision of the Carnegie Endowment for International Peace Division of International Law, 2 vols. (New York: Oxford, 1923) is useful.

During and immediately after the Nazi regime historians sought an explanation for Nazism in all aspects of German life. They made Hitler the lineal heir of such diverse men as Martin Luther and Frederick the Great because they worked from Hitler back. Examples of these include Rohan D'Olier Butler, *The Roots of National Socialism 1783-1933* (London: Faber and Faber, 1941); Carl Mayer, "On the Intellectual Origins of National Socialism," *Social Research IX (1942);* Hermann Rauschning, *The Conservative Revolution* (New York: Putnam, 1941); Peter Robert Edwin Viereck, *Metapolitics, from the Romantics to Hitler* (New York: Knopf, 1941). More objective studies have been written on German life and society by working from the past to the present. Such studies include William J. Bossenbrook, *The German Mind* (Detroit: Wayne State University Press, 1961); Georg G. Iggers, *The German Conception of History: The National Tradition of Historical Thought from Herder to the Present* (Middletown, Conn.: Wesleyan University Press, 1968); Hans Kohn, ed., *German History: Some New German Views* (Boston: Beacon Press, 1954); George L. Mosse, *The Crisis of German Ideology: Intellectual Origins of the Third Reich* (New York: Grosset and Dunlap, 1964); Fritz Stern, *The Politics of Cultural Despair: A Study in the Rise of the German Ideology* (Berkeley: University of California Press, 1961); Andrew G. Whiteside, "The Nature and Origins of National Socialism," *Journal of Central European Affairs* XVII (April, 1957).

In attempting to explain Hitler's rise to power, many historians examined the Weimar Republic and the failure of the German people to accept the Republic and its democratic origins. Works centering around the Republic include: Robert Clark, *The Fall of the German Republic, A Political Study* (New York: Russell and Russell, 1964); Ludwig Dehio, *German and World Politics in the Twentieth Century* (New York: Knopf, 1959, 1965); Andreas Dorpalen, *Hindenburg and the Weimar Republic* (Princeton: Princeton University Press, 1964); Peter Gay, *Weimar Culture: The Outsider as Insider* (New York: Harper, 1968); Calvin Hoover, *Germany Enters the Third Reich* (New York: Macmillan, 1933); Thomas Jarman, *The Rise and Fall of Nazi Germany* (New York: New York University Press, 1956); W. M. Knight-Patterson, *Germany: From Defeat to Conquest, 1913-1933* (London: Allen and Unwin, 1945); Eric G. Kollman, "Reinterpreting Modern German History: The Weimar Republic," *Journal of Central European Affairs,* XXI (1962); Elmer Luehr, *The New German Republic:*

The Reich in Transition (New York: Minton, Balch, 1929); Koppel Pinson, *Modern Germany: Its History and Civilization* (New York: Macmillan, 1966); Arthur Rosenberg, *A History of the German Republic,* translated by F. D. Morrow and L. Marie Sieveking (London: Methuen, 1936); Godfrey Scheele, *The Weimar Republic: Overture to the Third Reich* (London: Faber and Faber, 1946); George N. Shuster and Arnold Bergstraesser, *Germany, a Short History* (New York: Norton, 1944); Edmond Vermeil, *Germany in the Twentieth Century; A Political and Cultural History of the Weimar Republic and the Third Reich* (New York: Praeger, 1956); Oswald Villard, *The German Phoenix; The Story of the Republic* (New York: Smith and Haas, 1933).

A general history of the Weimar Republic did not satisfy other historians in explaining the rise of Hitler. These historians, instead, preferred to examine specific incidents within the Republic. The failure of the 1918 revolution to bring about any real change in Germany enticed historians to look here for the failure of democracy and the failure of the Republic. Among these are Werner T. Angress, *Stillborn Revolution: The Communist Bid for Power in Germany, 1921-1923* (Princeton: Princeton University Press, 1963); Rudolf Coper, *Failure of a Revolution; Germany in 1918-1919* (Cambridge: Cambridge University Press, 1955); Klaus Epstein, *Matthias Erzberger and the Dilemma of German Democracy* (Princeton: Princeton University Press, 1959); Ralph Lutz, *The German Revolution, 1918-1919* (Stanford: Stanford University Press, 1922); Ralph Lutz, ed., *Fall of the German Empire, 1914-1918* (Stanford: Stanford University Press, 1932); Robert Waite, *Vanguard of Nazism: The Free Corps Movement in Post-War Germany, 1918-1923* (Cambridge: Harvard University Press, 1952).

The military has drawn special attention for its role in preventing major change in German social life. Especially valuable are Hildegard R. Boeninger, "Hitler and the German Generals," *Journal of Central European Affairs,* XIV (April, 1954); Francis Carsten, *The Reichswehr and Politics: 1918-1933* (Oxford: Clarendon Press, 1966); Gordon Craig, "Reichswehr and National Socialism: The Policy of Wilhelm Groener, 1928-1932," *Political Science Quarterly,* LXIII (June, 1948); Harold J. Gordon, *The Reichswehr and the German Republic,* 1919-1926 (Princeton: Princeton University Press, 1957); Gerhard Ritter, "The Military and Politics in Germany," *Journal of Central European Affairs,* XVII (October, 1957).

Other historians, however, looked to the failure of the political parties as the explanation for the failure of democracy in Germany. See, for example, Attila Chanady, "The Disintegration of the German National Peoples' Party, 1924-1930," *Journal of Modern History,* XXXIX (March, 1967); Karl-Wilhelm Dahm, "German Protestantism and Politics, 1918-1939,"

Journal of Contemporary History, III (January, 1968); Ralf Dahrendorf, *Society and Democracy in Germany* (New York: Doubleday, 1967); Klaus Epstein, "The Zentrum Party in the Weimar Republic," *Journal of Modern History*, XXXIX (June, 1967); Konrad Heiden, *A History of National Socialism* (New York: Knopf, 1935); Lewis Hertzman, *DNVP: Right-Wing Opposition to the Weimar Republic, 1918-1924* (Lincoln: University of Nebraska Press, 1963); Walter Kaufmann, *Monarchism in the Weimar Republic* (New York: Bookman Associates, 1953); Klemens von Klemperer, *Germany's New Conservatism: Its History and Dilemma in the Twentieth Century* (Princeton: Princeton University Press, 1957); A. J. Nicholls, *Weimar and the Rise of Hitler* (London: Macmillan, 1968); Dietrich Orlow, "The Conversion of Myths into Political Power: The Case of the Nazi Party, 1925-1926," *American Historical Review*, LXXII (April, 1967); Dietrich Orlow, "The Organizational History and Structure of the NSDAP, 1919-23," *Journal of Modern History*, XXXVII (June, 1965); Reginald Phelps, "Hitler and the Deutsche Arbeiterpartei." *American Historical Review*, LXVIII (July, 1963); Frederick Watkins, *The Failure of Constitutional Emergency Powers under the German Republic* (Cambridge: Harvard University Press, 1939).

The economic disasters suffered by the Republic in 1923 and 1931 encouraged historians to emphasize the economic disillusionment of the Germans with the Republic. Useful examples are: James W. Angell, *The Recovery of Germany* (New Haven: Yale University Press, 1929); Edward W. Bennett, *Germany and the Diplomacy of the Financial Crisis, 1931* (Cambridge: Harvard University Press, 1962); Robert A. Brady, *The Rationalization Movement in German Industry* (Berkeley: University of California Press, 1933); Werner Bruck, *Social and Economic History of Germany from William II to Hitler, 1888-1938; A Comparative Study* (London: Oxford University Press, 1938); Waldo Chamberlin, *Industrial Relations in Germany 1914-1939* (Stanford: Stanford University Press, 1942); Gerald D. Feldman, "The Social and Economic Policies of German Big Business, 1918-1929," *American Historical Review*, LXXV (October, 1969); George W. Hallgarten, "Adolf Hitler and German Heavy Industry, 1931-1933," *Journal of Economic History*, XII (Summer, 1952); John Maynard Keynes, *The Economic Consequences of the Peace* (New York: Harcourt, Brace, 1920); Etienne Mantoux, *The Carthaginian Peace; or, The Economic Consequences of Mr. Keynes* (London, Oxford University Press, 1946); Ernst Nolte, "Big Business and German Politics: A Comment," *American Historical Review*, LXXV (October, 1969); Kenyon Poole, *German Financial Policies, 1932-1939* (Cambridge: Harvard University Press, 1939); Hjalmar Schacht, *The End of Reparations*, translated by Lewis

Gannett (New York: Jonathan Cape and Harrison Smith, 1931); Hjalmar Schacht, *The Stabilization of the Mark* (London: Allen and Unwin, 1927); Gustav Stolper, *German Economy, 1870-1940: Issues and Trends* (New York: Reynal and Hitchcock, 1940); John W. Wheeler-Bennett, *The Wreck of Reparations Being the Political Background of the Lausanne Agreement 1932* (New York: Morrow, 1933).

The importance of Hitler's personality cannot be overlooked in any explanation of why democracy failed in Germany. The most balanced account of Hitler's personal role in Nazi successes, and the best biography of Hitler is Alan Bullock, *Hitler: A Study in Tyranny,* rev. ed. (New York: Harper, 1962). An objective account by a German historian is found in Helmut Heiber, *Adolf Hitler; A Short Biography,* translated by Lawrence Wilson (London: O. Wolff, 1961). Facets of Hitler's life may be found in Martha Dodd, *Through Embassy Eyes* (New York: Harcourt, Brace, 1939); William E. Dodd, Jr., and Martha Dodd, *Ambassador Dodd's Diary* (New York: Harcourt, Brace, 1941); Klaus Epstein, "The Nazi Consolidation of Power," *Journal of Modern History,* XXXIV (March, 1962); Andre Francois-Poncet, *The Fateful Years; Memoirs of a French Ambassador in Berlin, 1931-1938,* translated by Jacques Le Clercq (New York: Harcourt, Brace, 1949); Oron J. Hale, "Adolf Hitler: Taxpayer," *American Historical Review,* LX (July, 1955); David Schoenbaum, *Hitler's Social Revolution: Class and Status in Nazi Germany, 1933-1939* (New York: Doubleday, 1966).

Accounts by contemporaries, some written in the period, others published as self-justification after Germany's defeat, reveal Hitler's charismatic appeal. Many of these provide insight into the German response to the man. Of these the best-known is Konrad Heiden, *Hitler; A Biography,* translated by Winifred Ray (New York: Knopf, 1936). Other valuable works include Otto Dietrich, *With Hitler on the Road to Power* (London: Lucas, 1934); Hermann Göring, *Political Testament of Hermann Göring: A Selection of Important Speeches and Articles,* translated by H. W. Blood-Ryan (London: Long, 1939); Franz von Papen, *Memoirs,* translated by Brian Connell (London: Andre Deutsch, 1952); Otto Strasser, *Hitler and I,* translated by Gwenda David and Eric Mosbacher (Boston: Houghton Mifflin, 1940); Fritz Thyssen, *I Paid Hitler* (New York: Farrar and Rinehart, 1941).

Historians have studied leading Germans other than Hitler in an effort to illuminate the phenomenon of Nazi success. The student might examine the following: Theodore Abel, *The Nazi Movement; Why Hitler Came to Power* (New York: Atherton Press, 1966); H. W. Blood-Ryan, *Franz von Papen; His Life and Times* (London: Rich and Cowan, 1940); Willi Frischauer, *Goering*

(London: Odhams, 1951); Curt Riess, *Joseph Goebbels* (New York: Doubleday, 1948); Amos E. Simpson, *Hjalmar Schacht in Perspective,* (The Hague: Mouton, 1969); Henry Turner, Jr., "Emil Kirdorf and the Nazi Party," *Central European History,* I (December, 1968); John W. Wheeler-Bennett, *Wooden Titan; Hindenburg in Twenty Years of German History, 1914-1934* (New York: Morrow, 1936).